Subsidia et Instrumenta Linguarum Orientis

(SILO)

Herausgegeben von / Edited by
Reinhard G. Lehmann / Robert M. Kerr

5

2012
Harrassowitz Verlag · Wiesbaden

Konrad Volk

A Sumerian Chrestomathy

With the collaboration of Silvano Votto
and Jessica Baldwin

2012
Harrassowitz Verlag · Wiesbaden

Cover illustration:
Découvertes en Chaldée par E. de Sarzec, ouvrage accompagné de planches, publié par les soins de L. Heuzey, avec le concours de A. Amiaud et F. Thureau-Dangin pour la partie épigraphique.
Second volume: Partie épigraphique et planches (Paris 1884–1912), pl. XLV.

Bibliografische Information der Deutschen Nationalbibliothek
Die Deutsche Nationalbibliothek verzeichnet diese Publikation in der Deutschen Nationalbibliografie; detaillierte bibliografische Daten sind im Internet über http://dnb.d-nb.de abrufbar.

Bibliographic information published by the Deutsche Nationalbibliothek
The Deutsche Nationalbibliothek lists this publication in the Deutsche Nationalbibliografie; detailed bibliographic data are available in the internet at http://dnb.d-nb.de.

For further information about our publishing program consult our website http://www.harrassowitz-verlag.de

Printed on permanent/durable paper.
Logo: Semitic inscription on the top of a foundation nail. Period of the Amorite Kingdoms (2004–1595 BCE). Larsa, Babylon. © akg-images/Erich Lessing.
Printing and binding: docupoint, Magdeburg
Printed in Germany

ISSN 1867-8165
ISBN 978-3-447-06782-9

To the memory of

Johannes Jacobus Adrianus van Dijk

(28.1.1915 – 14.5.1996)

and

Hermann Behrens SCJ

(15.7.1944 – 2.8.1996)

teacher and friend

Contents

Preface

A Sumerian Chrestomathy contains 44 texts of varying contents: royal inscriptions, legal, and economic documents. For pedagogic reasons literary texts are not included. Some texts are accompanied by a transliteration and/or a version in Neo-Assyrian script, so that the students can learn the Neo-Assyrian forms, which are of fundamental importance for the use of the sign list in this book and, in general, for most Assyriological sign lists.

Each inscription is to be studied with the help of the sign list, the list of phonetic values, and the glossary. In this *A Sumerian Chrestomathy* I have intentionally not dealt with questions of grammar. Instead, the reader is referred to three rather recent publications on the subject: P. Attinger, *Éléments de linguistique sumérienne. La construction de* du_{11}*/e/di «dire»* (Fribourg/Göttingen 1993 [= Orbis Biblicus et Orientalis; Sonderband]); D.O. Edzard, *Sumerian Grammar* (Leiden/Boston 2003 [= Handbook of Oriental Studies. Section 1, Near and Middle East, vol. 71]); A.H. Jagersma, *A Descriptive Grammar of Sumerian* (https://openaccess.leidenuniv.nl/handle/1887/16107).

For a general introduction to Sumerology, W.H.Ph. Römer, *Die Sumerologie. Einführung in die Forschung und Bibliographie in Auswahl* (Münster 1999 [= Alter Orient und Altes Testament 262]) is highly recommended.

This book began as a manuscript called "*Sumerische Chrestomathie. Texte zusammengestellt, teilweise transkribiert, in neuassyrische Zeichenformen übertragen und mit Glossar und Zeichenliste versehen*" (Eschbach 1978). It proved to be a very useful and much requested tool for many beginners. Over the years, a good number of both teachers and students who used my *Sumerische Chrestomathie* gave me their personal notes, corrections, and improvements, for which I am very grateful. I would like to thank the following persons for providing such help: P. Attinger; J. Bauer; H. Behrens; J.S. Cooper; J.J.A. van Dijk; D.O. Edzard; D. Foxvog; M.J. Geller; J. Keetman; B. Kienast; W.G. Lambert; W.R. Mayer; H. Neumann; G. Rubio; W. Sallaberger; G.J. Selz; H. Steible; M.P. Streck; C. Wilcke; A. Zgoll.

Fr. Silvano Votto S.J. not only translated the entire manuscript into English but also made a considerable number of improvements. I owe him very special thanks for his invaluable contributions to this book.

During the preparation of *A Sumerian Chrestomathy* André Volk digitized the hand-drawn sign list. Jessica Baldwin was kind enough to assist me in the various stages of updating the manuscript and also made a number of very useful suggestions. Last but not least, I am most grateful to Jana Matuszak for her help in proofreading, to Dr. Barbara Krauß and Julia Guthmüller (Harrassowitz Verlag) for their support in the making of *A Sumerian Chrestomathy,* and to Gerlinde Hoferer-Volk for editing this book in its current format.

Tübingen 2012 Konrad Volk

Bibliographic Abbreviations

With some exceptions and additions, bibliographic abbreviations follow the standard abbreviations in the *Assyrian Dictionary of the Oriental Institute of the University of Chicago* (Chicago/Glückstadt 1956ff.), W. von Soden, *Akkadisches Handwörterbuch* (Wiesbaden 1958-81), and *The Sumerian Dictionary of the University Museum of the University of Pennsylvania*, edited by Å.W. Sjöberg (Philadelphia 1984ff.). A useful list of bibliographic abbreviations can also be found in the *Reallexikon der Assyriologie* 12 (Berlin/Boston 2009-2011) III-XLVIII.

AcOr	Acta Orientalia (Copenhagen 1922ff.)
AEM I/1	J.-M. Durand, Archives épistolaires de Mari I/1 (Paris 1988)
AfO	Archiv für Orientforschung, vols. 3ff. [vols. 1-2 = AfK] (Berlin, Graz and Horn 1926ff.)
AnOr	Analecta Orientalia (Rome 1931ff.)
AOAT	Alter Orient und Altes Testament. Veröffentlichungen zur Kultur und Geschichte des Alten Orients und des Alten Testaments (Kevelaer/Neukirchen-Vluyn, Münster 1969ff.)
AoF	Altorientalische Forschungen (Berlin 1974ff.)
AoN	J. Bauer, Altorientalistische Notizen (Würzburg 1976ff.)
AS	Assyriological Studies (Chicago 1931ff.)
ASJ	Acta Sumerologica Japonica (Hiroshima 1979ff.)
AulOr	Aula Orientalis (Sabadell [Barcelona] 1983ff.)
AWL	J. Bauer, Altsumerische Wirtschaftstexte aus Lagaš (= St.Pohl 9 [1972])
Babylon	E. Cancik-Kirschbaum/M. van Ess /J. Marzahn (eds.), Babylon. Wissenskultur in Orient und Okzident. Topoi. Berlin Studies of the Ancient World (Berlin/Boston 2011)
BaF	Baghdader Forschungen (Mainz 1979ff.)
BaM	Baghdader Mitteilungen (Berlin 1960ff.)
BCSMS	Bulletin of the Canadian Society for Mesopotamian Studies (Toronto 1981ff.)
BFE	M. Krebernik, Die Beschwörungen aus Fara und Ebla. Untersuchungen zur ältesten keilschriftlichen Beschwörungsliteratur (Hildesheim/Zürich/New York 1984)
BiOr	Bibliotheca Orientalis (Leiden 1943ff.)
BSA	Bulletin on Sumerian Agriculture (Cambridge [U.K.] 1984ff.)
CAD	The Assyrian Dictionary of the Oriental Institute of the University of Chicago (Chicago/Glückstadt 1956ff.)
Care of the Elderly	M. Stol/S.P. Vleeming (eds.), The Care of the Elderly in the Ancient Near East (= Studies in the History and Culture of the Ancient Near East XIV [Leiden/Boston/Köln 1998])

CDOG	Colloquien der Deutschen Orient-Gesellschaft (Saarbrücken 1997-2004; Wiesbaden 2008ff.)
CIRPL	E. Sollberger, Corpus des inscriptions 'royales' présargoniques de Lagaš (Genève 1956)
clergé	D. Charpin, Le clergé d'Ur au siècle d'Hammurabi (XIXe-XVIIIe siècles av. J.-C.) (Genève/Paris 1986)
CM	Cuneiform Monographs (Groningen 1992ff.)
CRRA	Compte rendu de la ...[e] Rencontre Assyriologique Internationale (1951ff.)
CT	Cuneiform Texts from Babylonian Tablets in the British Museum (London 1896ff.)
Cultic Calendars	M.E. Cohen, The Cultic Calendars of the Ancient Near East (Bethesda 1993)
CUSAS	Cornell University Studies in Assyriology and Sumerology (Bethesda 2007ff.)
DC	Découvertes en Chaldée par E. de Sarzec, ouvrage accompagné de planches, publié par les soins de L. Heuzey, avec le concours de A. Amiaud et F. Thureau-Dangin pour la partie épigraphique. Premier volume: texte (Paris 1884-1912). Second volume: Partie épigraphique et planches (Paris 1884-1912)
DV 3/II	M.V. Nikolskij, Dokumenty chozjajstvennoj otčetnosti drevnejšej epochi Chaldei iz sobranija N.P. Lichačeva. Drevnosti Vostočnyja Trudy Vostočnoj Komissii Imperatorskago Moskovskago Archeologičeskago Obščestva 3/II (St. Petersburg 1908)
EANEL	C. Wilcke, Early Ancient Near Eastern Law. A History of Its Beginnings. The Early Dynastic and Sargonic Periods (Winona Lake 2007)
ECTJ	A. Westenholz, Early Cuneiform Texts in Jena. (København 1975)
ÉLS	P. Attinger, Éléments de linguistique sumérienne. La construction de du_{11}/e/di «dire» (Fribourg/Göttingen 1993 [= OBO; Sonderband])
Épithètes royales	M.-J. Seux, Épithètes royales akkadiennes et sumériennes (Paris 1967)
Familiengründung	C. Wilcke, Familiengründung im Alten Babylonien. In: Geschlechtsreife und Legitimation zur Zeugung (= Kindheit Jugend Familie I, E.W. Müller, ed.). Veröffentlichungen des Instituts für Historische Anthropologie 3 (Freiburg/München 1985) 213-317
FAOS	Freiburger altorientalische Studien (Wiesbaden, Stuttgart 1975ff.)

FI	M. Civil, The Farmer's Instructions. A Sumerian Agricultural Manual. Aula Orientalis – Supplementa 5 (Sabadell [Barcelona] 1994)
Fö	W. Förtsch, Altbabylonische Wirtschaftstexte aus der Zeit Lugalanda's und Urukagina's (VS 14/1, Leipzig 1916)
Fossey	Ch. Fossey, Manuel d'Assyriologie, Tome II. Évolution des cunéiformes (Paris 1926)
FT	H. de Genouillac, Fouilles de Tello (Paris 1934-1936)
Gazetteer	'*Gazetteer of Ceremonial Names*'. pp. 63-161 in A.R. George, House Most High. The Temples of Ancient Mesopotamia (= MC 5 [1993])
Gedenkschrift R. Kutscher	A.F. Rainey et al. (eds.), *kinattūtu ša dārâti*. Raphael Kutscher Memorial Volume (Tel Aviv 1993)
HANE/S	History of the Ancient Near East/Studies (Padova 1990ff.)
HdO	Handbuch der Orientalistik (Leiden 1948ff.)
HSAO	Heidelberger Studien zum Alten Orient – A. Falkenstein zum 17. September 1966 (Wiesbaden 1967)
HUCA	Hebrew Union College Annual (Cincinnati 1924ff.)
Iraq	Iraq. Published by the British School of Archaeology in Iraq (London 1934ff.)
Ist.Mitt.	Istanbuler Mitteilungen. Herausgegeben vom Deutschen Archäologischen Institut, Abteilung Istanbul (Istanbul and Tübingen 1933ff.)
ITT	Inventaire des tablettes de Tello conservées au Musée Impérial Ottoman (Paris 1910-1921)
JAOS	Journal of the American Oriental Society (New Haven 1893ff.)
JCS	Journal of Cuneiform Studies (New Haven, Cambridge [Mass.], Philadelphia, Baltimore 1947ff.)
JNES	Journal of Near Eastern Studies (Chicago 1942ff.)
Kaskal	Kaskal. Rivista di storia, ambiente e culture del Vicino Oriente antico (Padua 2004ff.)
LAK	A. Deimel, Liste der archaischen Keilschriftzeichen von Fara (= WVDOG 40 [1922])
LIH	L.W. King, The Letters and Inscriptions of Hammurabi (London 1898-1900)
MC	Mesopotamian Civilizations (Winona Lake 1989ff.)
Mesopotamia	1. Mesopotamia. Rivista di Archeologia (Torino 1966ff.) 2. Mesopotamia. Copenhagen Studies in Assyriology (Copenhagen 1972ff.)
MesZL	R. Borger, Mesopotamisches Zeichenlexikon (= AOAT 305 [2004; ^{2}2010])
MSL	Materialien zum sumerischen Lexikon (Rome 1937ff.)

N.A.B.U.	Nouvelles Assyriologiques Brèves et Utilitaires (Rouen/Paris 1987ff.)
NG	A. Falkenstein, Die neusumerischen Gerichtsurkunden (München 1956-1957)
OA	Oriens Antiquus. Rivista del Centro per le Antichità e la Storia dell'Arte del Vicino Oriente (Roma 1962ff.)
OBC	Orientalia Biblica et Christiana (Glückstadt/Wiesbaden 1991ff.)
OBO	Orbis Biblicus et Orientalis (Freiburg [Schweiz] 1973ff.)
OIP	Oriental Institute Publications (Chicago 1924ff.)
OPSNKF	Occasional Publications of the Samuel Noah Kramer Fund (Philadelphia 1988ff.)
OrAntMisc	Orientis Antiqui Miscellanea (Roma 1994ff.)
OrNS	Orientalia. Nova Series (Rom 1932ff.)
OrSc	Orientalia Suecana (Uppsala/Stockholm 1952ff.)
PEa	PROTO-Ea (Nippur Recension). In: MSL XIV (Rome 1979) 30-63
PPAC 1	Z. Yang, Sargonic Inscriptions from Adab. The Institute for the History of Ancient Civilisations, Periodic Publications on Ancient Civilisations 1 (Changchun 1989)
PSD	Å.W. Sjöberg (ed.), The Sumerian Dictionary of the University Museum of the University of Pennsylvania (Philadelphia 1984ff.)
RGTC	Répertoire géographique des textes cunéiformes. Beihefte zum Tübinger Atlas des Vorderen Orients, Series B (Wiesbaden 1974ff.)
RIME	The Royal Inscriptions of Mesopotamia, Early Periods (Toronto 1990ff.)
RlA	Reallexikon der Assyriologie (Berlin/Leipzig and Berlin/New York 1932ff.)
SANTAG	K. Hecker/W. Sommerfeld (eds.), SANTAG. Arbeiten und Untersuchungen zur Keilschriftkunde (Wiesbaden 1990ff.)
SARI	J.S. Cooper, Sumerian and Akkadian Royal Inscriptions I: Presargonic Inscriptions (New Haven 1986)
SAZ	A. Cavigneaux, Die sumerisch-akkadischen Zeichenlisten: Überlieferungsprobleme (Ph.Diss. München 1976)
SEL	Studi epigrafici e linguistici sul Vicino Oriente antico (Verona 1984ff.)
SKLy	J. Krecher, Sumerische Kultlyrik (Wiesbaden 1966)
SRU	D.O. Edzard, Sumerische Rechtsurkunden des III. Jahrtausends aus der Zeit vor der III. Dynastie von Ur (München 1968)
St.Pohl	Studia Pohl (Rom 1967ff.)
St.Pohl SM	Studia Pohl: Series Maior (Rom 1969ff.)
St.Sem.Ups.	Studia Semitica Upsaliensia (Uppsala 1968ff.)

Studies Birot	J.-M. Durand/J.-R. Kupper (eds.), Miscellanea Babylonica. Mélanges offerts à Maurice Birot (Paris 1985)
Studies Borger	S.M. Maul (ed.), *Tikip santakki mala bašmu...* Festschrift für Rykle Borger zu seinem 65. Geburtstag am 24. Mai 1994 (= CM 10 [1998])
Studies Diakonoff	M.A. Dandamaev et al. (eds.), Societies and Languages of the Ancient Near East. Studies in Honour of I.M. Diakonoff (Warminster 1982)
Studies Hallo	M.E. Cohen et al. (eds.), The Tablet and the Scroll. Near Eastern Studies in honour of William W. Hallo (Bethesda 1993)
Studies Kienast	G.J. Selz (ed.), Festschrift für B. Kienast zu seinem 70. Geburtstage dargebracht von Freunden, Schülern und Kollegen (= AOAT 274 [2003])
Studies Klein	Y. Sefati et al. (eds.), "An Experienced Scribe who Neglects Nothing". Ancient Near Eastern Studies in Honor of Jacob Klein (Bethesda 2005)
Studies Matouš	B. Hruška/G. Komoróczy (eds.), Festschrift Lubor Matouš (Budapest 1978)
Studies Sjöberg	H. Behrens/D. Loding/M.T. Roth (eds.), DUMU-E2-DUB-BA-A. Studies in Honor of Åke W. Sjöberg (= OPSNKF 11 [1989])
Studies Tadmor	M. Cogan/I. Eph'al (eds.), Ah, Assyria ... Studies in Assyrian History and Ancient Near Eastern Historiography, presented to Hayim Tadmor. (Jerusalem 1991)
Studies Wilcke	W. Sallaberger/K. Volk/A. Zgoll (eds.), Literatur, Politik und Recht in Mesopotamien. Festschrift für Claus Wilcke (= OBC 14 [2003])
Sumer	Sumer. A Journal of Archaeology and History in Iraq. The Republic of Iraq. Directorate General of Antiquities (Baghdad 1945ff.)
TCS	Texts from Cuneiform Sources (Locust Valley [New York] 1966ff.)
ThŠH	J. Klein, Three Šulgi Hymns. Sumerian Royal Hymns Glorifying King Šulgi of Ur (Ramat-Gan 1981)
TMH(NF)	Texte und Materialien der Frau Prof. Hilprecht Collection of Babylonian Antiquities (Neue Folge: Leipzig/Berlin 1932ff.)
TUAT (NF)	Texte aus der Umwelt des Alten Testaments (Gütersloh 1982ff.); NF (Gütersloh 2004ff.)
UET	Ur Excavations, Texts (London 1928ff.)
UGASL	G.J. Selz, Untersuchungen zur Götterwelt des altsumerischen Stadtstaates von Lagaš (= OPSNKF 13 [1995])

UVB	Uruk. Vorläufiger Bericht über die von dem Deutschen Archäologischen Institut und der Deutschen Orient-Gesellschaft aus Mitteln der Deutschen Forschungsgemeinschaft unternommenen Ausgrabungen in Uruk-Warka (Berlin 1930ff.)
VA	Siglum of the *V*orderasiatische *A*bteilung of the Vorderasiatisches Museum, Berlin
VS	Vorderasiatische Schriftdenkmäler der Königlichen/Staatlichen Museen zu Berlin (Leipzig, Berlin 1907ff.)
WO	Die Welt des Orients (Wuppertal, Stuttgart and Göttingen 1947ff.)
WVDOG	Wissenschaftliche Veröffentlichungen der Deutschen Orient-Gesellschaft (Leipzig, Berlin 1901ff.)
Xenia	Xenia. Konstanzer Althistorische Vorträge und Forschungen (W. Schuller ed., Konstanz 1981ff.)
YOS	Yale Oriental Series, Babylonian Texts (New Haven 1915ff.)
ZA(NF)	Zeitschrift für Assyriologie (Leipzig, Berlin, Straßburg 1886ff.; Neue Folge: Berlin/Leipzig, Berlin, Berlin/New York 1924ff.)
ZABR	Zeitschrift für altorientalische und biblische Rechtsgeschichte (Wiesbaden 1995ff.)

List of Texts

The number of each text is accompanied by the original publication of the copy reproduced in this book and by its most recent edition.

I. Royal Inscriptions

1. CT XXI, pl. 3, No. 90015 (brick); D.R. Frayne, RIME 3/2, 69-71 ('Ur-Nammu E3/2.1.1.33')
2. YOS IX 14 (clay nail); D.O. Edzard, RIME 3/1, 113 ('Gudea E3/1.1.7.8')
3. CT XXI, pl. 2, No. 90009 (brick); D.R. Frayne, RIME 3/2, 25f. ('Ur-Nammu E3/2.1.1.4')
4. VS I 22, VA 57 (brick); D.O. Edzard, RIME 3/1, 156 ('Gudea E3/1.1.7.64')
5. CT XXI, pl. 36, No. 90289 (brick); D.O. Edzard, RIME 3/1, 154f. ('Gudea E3/1.1.7.62')
6. CT XXI, pl. 37, No. 90288 (brick); D.O. Edzard, RIME 3/1, 120f. ('Gudea E3/1.1.7.18')
7. OIP 14 33 (brick); D.O. Edzard, RIME 3/1, 135f. ('Gudea E3/1.1.7.37')
8. VS I 23, VA 3129 (brick); D.O. Edzard, RIME 3/1, 141f. ('Gudea E3/1.1.7.44')
9. VS 1 21, VA 55 (brick); D.O. Edzard, RIME 3/1, 130f. ('Gudea E3/1.1.7.31')
10. FT II, pl. XXXIX, TG 2429 (stone tablet); D.O. Edzard, RIME 3/1, 109f. ('Gudea E3/1.1.7.4')
11. DC II, pl. XLVI (door socket); D.R. Frayne, RIME 1, 211 ('En-metena E1.9.5.10')
12. CIRPL 1, Urn. 3 (copper nail); D.R. Frayne, RIME 1, 93f. ('Ur-Nanše E1.9.1.7')
13. DC II, pl. LVI (door socket); D.R. Frayne, RIME 1, 216f. ('En-metena E1.9.5.14')
14. CIRPL 36, Ent. 27 (door socket); D.R. Frayne, RIME 1, 224f. ('En-metena E1.9.5.20')
15. DC II, pl. XLVI; photo: DC I, pl. 31bis, 3 (brick); D.R. Frayne, RIME 1, 173f. ('En-anatum I E1.9.4.3')
16. DC II, pl. XLV (brick); D.R. Frayne, RIME 1, 156-158 ('E-anatum E1.9.3.9')
17. CIRPL 59, Ukg. 17 (clay olive); H. Steible, FAOS 5/1, 338f. ('Uru'inimgina 17')
18. CIRPL 56, Ukg. 10 (stone tablet); D.R. Frayne, RIME 1, 279f. ('URU-KA-gina E1.9.9.6')
19. CIRPL 45, En. II 1 (door socket); D.R. Frayne, RIME 1, 237f. ('En-anatum II E1.9.6.1')
20. CIRPL 36, Ent. 26 (door socket); D.R. Frayne, RIME 1, 226f. ('En-metena E1.9.5.23')
21. CIRPL 32, Ent. 1 (diorite statue); photo: UET 1, pl. A-B; D.R. Frayne, RIME 1, 219-222 ('En-metena E1.9.5.17'); G. Marchesi/N. Marchetti, MC 14, 176-179

22. DC II, pl. VI-VII (diorite statue, "petite statue debout"); photo: F. Johansen, Mesopotamia 6, pl. 1-4; D.O. Edzard, RIME 3/1, 29f. ('Gudea E3/1.1.7.StA')
23. DC II, pl. XVI-XVII (diorite statue, "statue dite aux épaules étroites"); photo: F. Johansen, Mesopotamia 6, pl. 5-8; D.O. Edzard, RIME 3/1, 38-40 ('Gudea E3/1.1.7.StC')
24. DC II, pl. XVII-XIX (diorite statue, "statue colossale"); photo: F. Johansen, Mesopotamia 6, pl. 23-27; D.O. Edzard, RIME 3/1, 40-42 ('Gudea E3/1.1.7.StD')
25. DC II, pl. XXIII-XXV (diorite statue, "l'architecte à la règle"); photo: F. Johansen, Mesopotamia 6, pl. 28-32; D.O. Edzard, RIME 3/1, 46-48 ('Gudea E3/1.1.7.StF')
26. DC II, pl. XXVIII (diorite statue, "petite statue assise, acéphale"); photo: F. Johansen, Mesopotamia 6, pl. 33-36; D.O. Edzard, RIME 3/1, 50f. ('Gudea E3/1.1.7.StH')
27. UVB 10, pl. 28 (door socket); D.R. Frayne, RIME 3/2, 262-264 ('Amar-Suena E3/2.1.3.16')
28. LIH 58 (shaft); D.R. Frayne, RIME 4, 347-349 ('Ḫammu-rāpi E4.3.6.12')
29. UET 8 84 (cone head); D.R. Frayne, RIME 4, 278f. ('Rīm-Sîn I E4.2.14.6')

II. Legal Documents

30. OIP 14 192 (clay tablet); Z. Yang, PPAC 1, 119f.; 346f. (loan of silver)
31. TMHNF 1/2 24 (clay tablet); R.K. Englund, CDOG 4, 127; 148 (loan of silver)
32. JCS 8 (1954) 46 (clay tablet); A. Falkenstein, NG 2, 1f. (marriage decree)
33. DV 3/II 293 (clay tablet); G.J. Selz, FAOS 15/1, 521f. (purchase of slaves and workers)
34. DV 3/II 17 (clay tablet); D.O. Edzard, SRU, 93f. (purchase of a cult singer)
35. TMH 5 216 (clay tablet); D.O. Edzard, SRU, 127; A. Westenholz, ECTJ 99 (guarantee)
36. TMHNF 1/2 259 (clay tablet); A. Falkenstein, NG 2, 212f. (record of an oath)
37. NG III, Tf. 2 (clay tablet); A. Falkenstein, NG 2, 27f.; H. Neumann, TUAT NF 1, 2f. (suit for breach of betrothal promise)
38. ITT 3/2, pl. 21, 5279 (clay tablet); A. Falkenstein, NG 2, 159-163; C. Wilcke, Care of the Elderly, 50f. (claim of property and a slave; liberation of the daughters of this slave)
39. ZA 55 (1962) 71 (clay tablet); for this controversial document see S. Greengus, HUCA 40-41 (1969-1970) 33-44; J. van Dijk, OrNS 39 (1970) 99-102; Å. Sjöberg, ibid. 92; M. Roth, JAOS 103 (1983) 278 ad 24; H. Lutzmann, TUAT 1, 198; J.-M. Durand, AEM I/1, 525 b); C. Wilcke, Xenia 32 (1992) 70, note 25 (decree of divorce); H. Neumann, ZABR 10 (2004) 71-92; M. Civil, CUSAS 17, 263

III. Economic Documents

40. VS 14/1 44 (clay tablet); J. Bauer, AWL, 281f. (delivery of fodder)
41. VS 14/1 128 (clay tablet); J. Bauer, AWL, 324 (delivery of animal products for a festival)
42. VS 14/1 35 (clay tablet); J. Bauer, AWL, 289f. (account of sheep and goats)
43. VS 14/1 145 (clay tablet); J. Bauer, AWL, 296f. (purchase and branding of a steer)
44. VS 14/1 94 (clay tablet); J. Bauer, AWL 452-455 (offering of beer to the gods)

Supplementary materials such as photographs of the objects, corrections, and additional material can be found at http://www.ianes.uni-tuebingen.de/sumerianchrestomathy

1. Texts 1 - 44

1

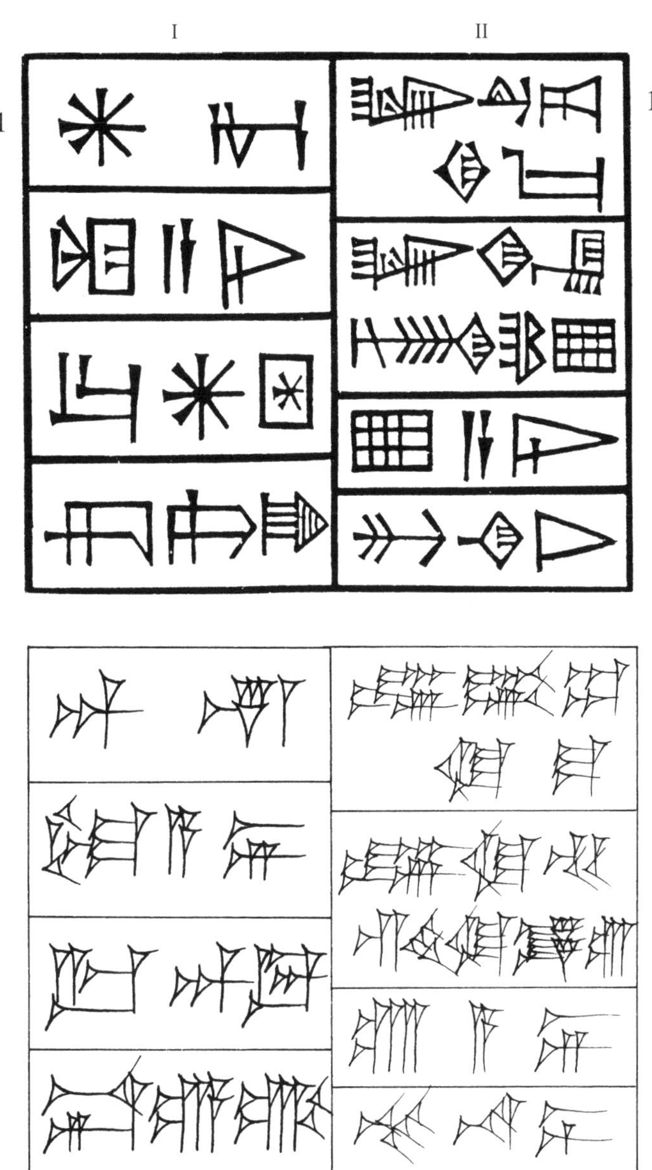

^{d}inana / nin-a-ni / ur-^{d}namma / ninta kala-ga / lugal uri$_{5}$(ŠEŠ.AB)^{ki}-ma / lugal ki-en-gi ki-uri-ke$_{4}$ / é-a-ni / mu-na-dù

2

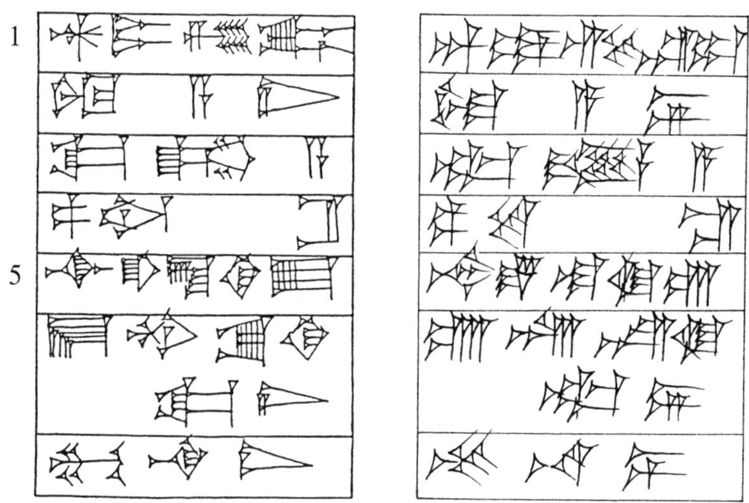

^{d}dumu-zi-abzu(ZU.AB) / nin-a-ni / gù-dé-a / énsi(PA.TE.SI) / lagas(NU$_{11}$.BUR.LA)^{ki}-ke$_{4}$ / é g̃ír-su^{ki}-ka-ni / mu-na-dù

3

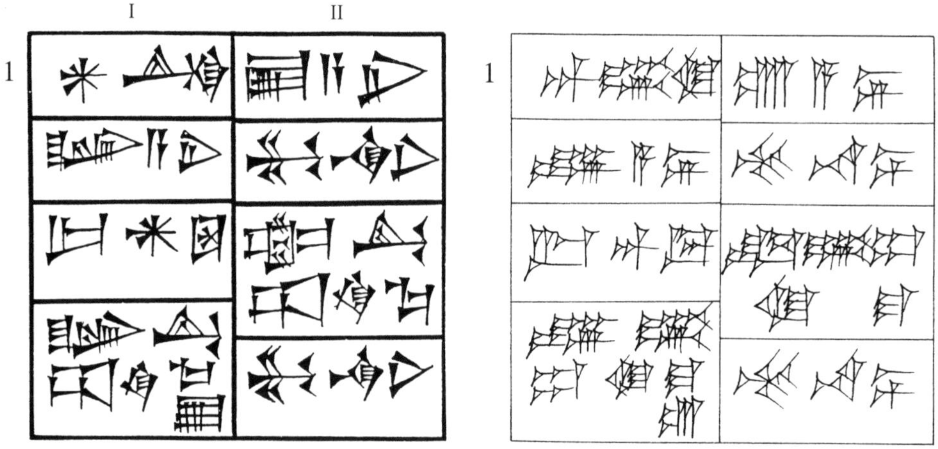

^{d}nanna(ŠEŠ.KI) / lugal-a-ni / ur-^{d}namma / lugal uri$_{5}$(ŠEŠ.AB)^{ki}-ma-ke$_{4}$ / é-a-ni / mu-na-dù / bàd uri$_{5}$(ŠEŠ.AB)^{ki}-ma / mu-na-dù

4

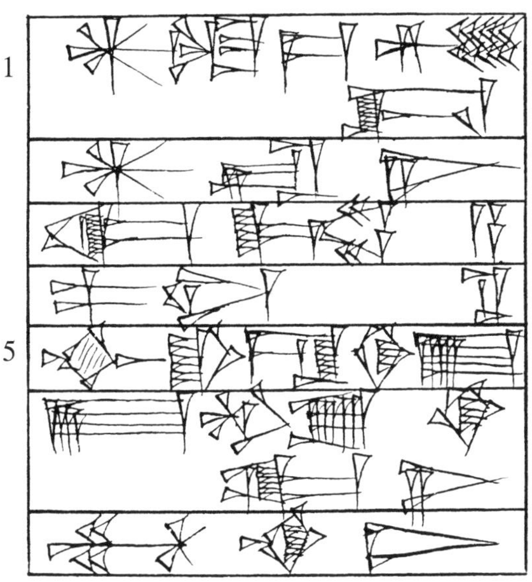

^{d}nin-ĝeš-zi-da / diĝir-ra-ni / gù-dé-a / énsi(PA.TE.SI) / lagas(⸢NU$_{11}$⸣.BUR.LA)^{ki}-ke$_{4}$ / é ĝír-su^{ki}-ka-ni / mu-na-dù

5

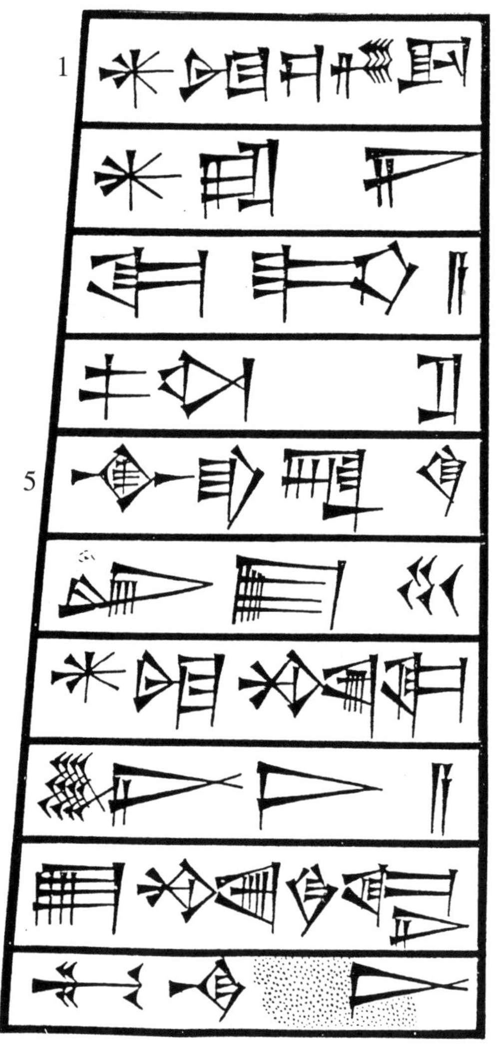

6

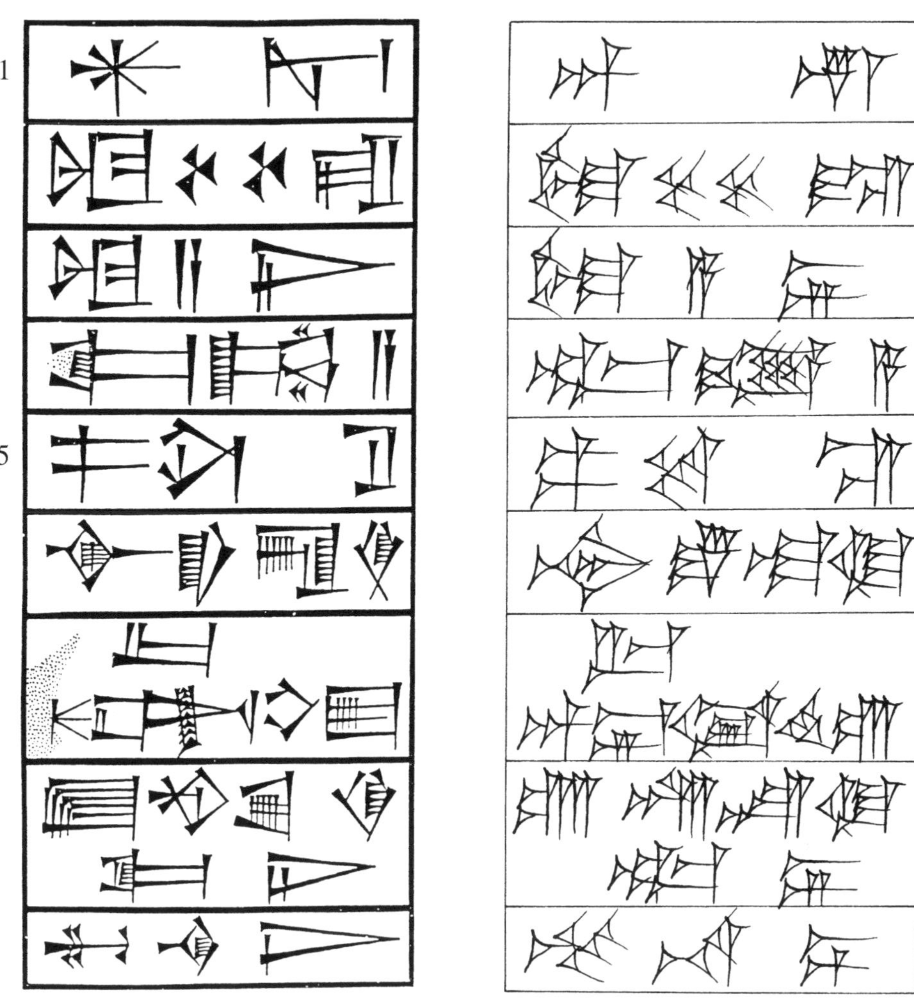

^{d}inana / nin kur-kur-ra / nin-a-ni / gù-dé-a / énsi(PA.TE.SI) / lagas(NU$_{11}$.BUR.LA)^{ki} / ur ⸢^{d}⸣ĝá-tùm-du$_{10}$-ke$_{4}$ / é ĝír-su^{ki}-ka-ni / mu-na-dù

7

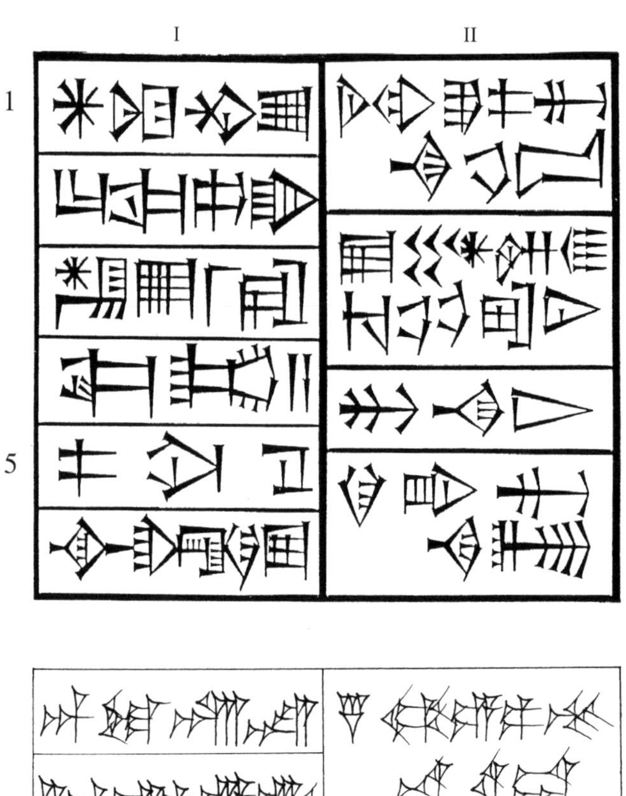

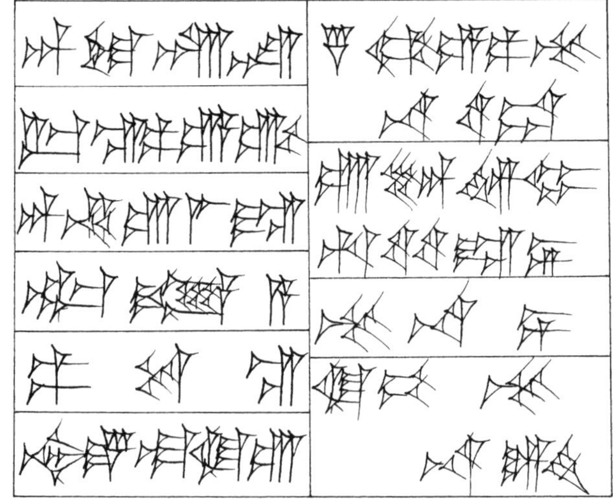

^{d}nin-ĝír-su / ur-saĝ kala-ga / ^{d}en-líl-lá-ra / gù-dé-a / énsi(PA.TE.SI) / lagas(NU$_{11}$.BUR.LA)^{ki}-ke$_{4}$ / níĝ-ul-e pa mu-na-è(UD.DU) / é-ninnu-ánzu(AN.IM.MI)^{mušen}-bábbar-ra-ni / mu-na-dù / ki-bé mu-na-ge$_{4}$

8

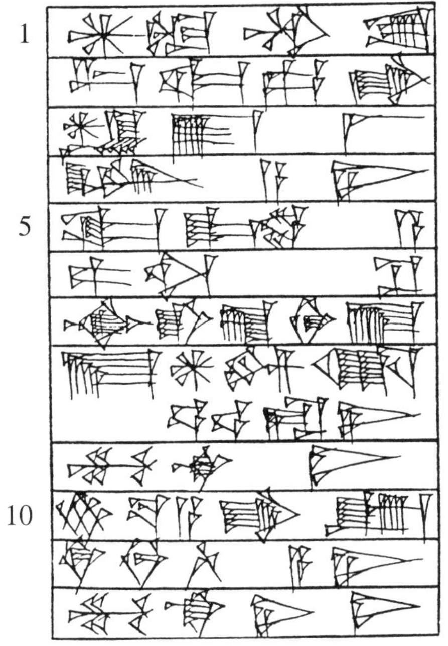

9

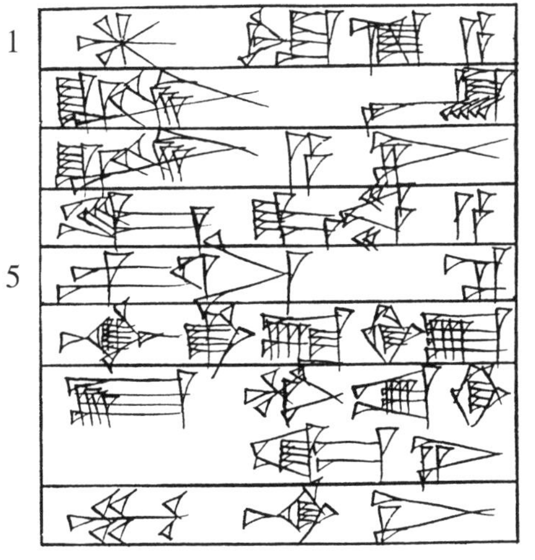

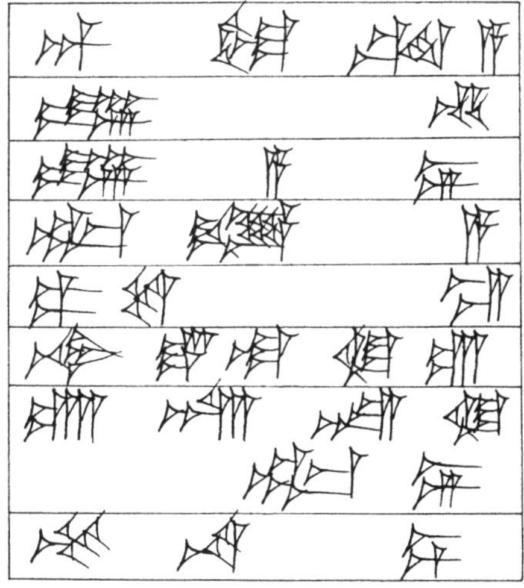

10

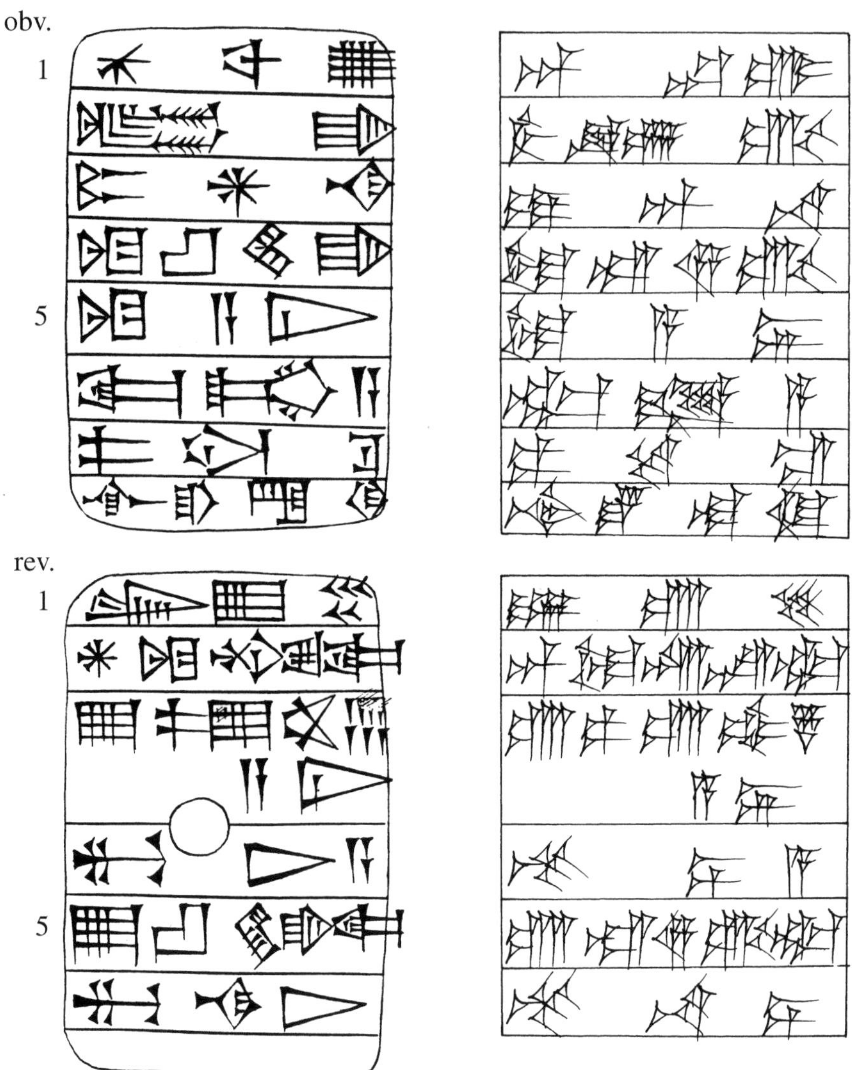

^{d}ba-Ú / munus sa$_6$-ga / dumu an-na / nin iri-kù-ga / nin-a-ni / gù-dé-a / énsi(PA.TE.SI) / lagas(NU$_{11}$.BUR.LA)^{ki} / lú é-ninnu / ^{d}nin-g̃ír-su-ka / é-g̃idru é ub ⌜umun$_7$⌝-a-ni / mu-dù-a / é iri-kù-ga-ka<-ni> / mu-na-dù

11

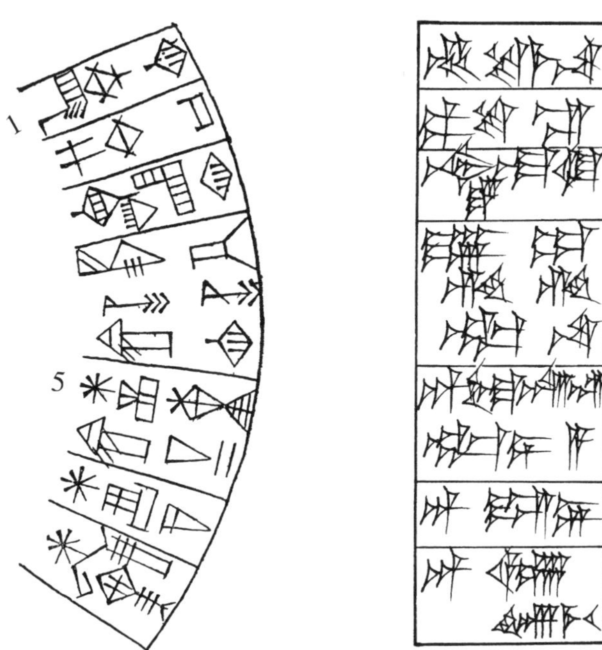

en-te:me-na / énsi(PA.TE.SI) / lagas(NU$_{11}$.BUR.LA)^{ki} / lú èš-gi gi-gù-na / ^{d}nin-g̃ír-sú-ka dù-a / dig̃ir-ra-ni / ^{d}sul-luḫša

12

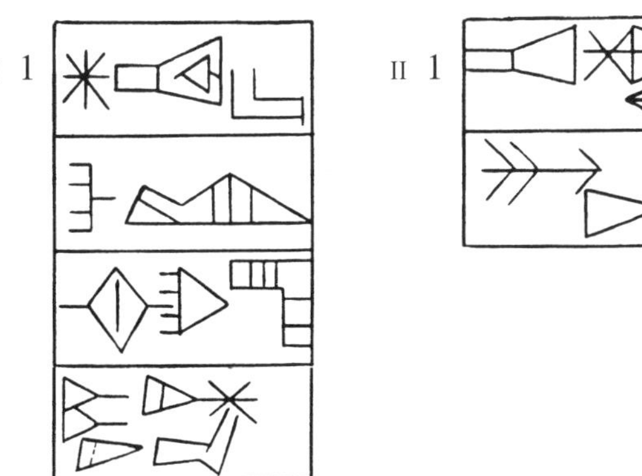

13

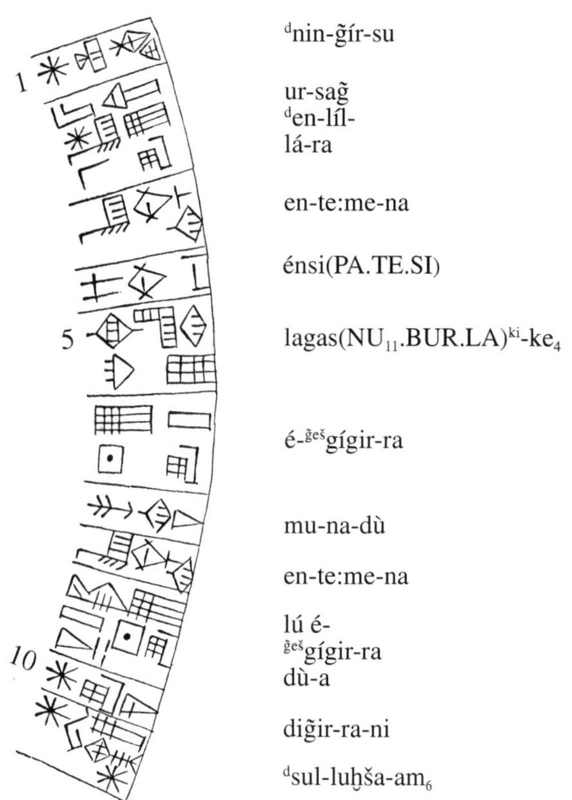

^{d}nin-ĝír-su

ur-saĝ
^{d}en-líl-
lá-ra

en-te:me-na

énsi(PA.TE.SI)

lagas(NU$_{11}$.BUR.LA)^{ki}-ke$_{4}$

é-^{ĝeš}gígir-ra

mu-na-dù

en-te:me-na

lú é-
^{ĝeš}gígir-ra
dù-a

diĝir-ra-ni

^{d}sul-luḫša-am$_{6}$

14

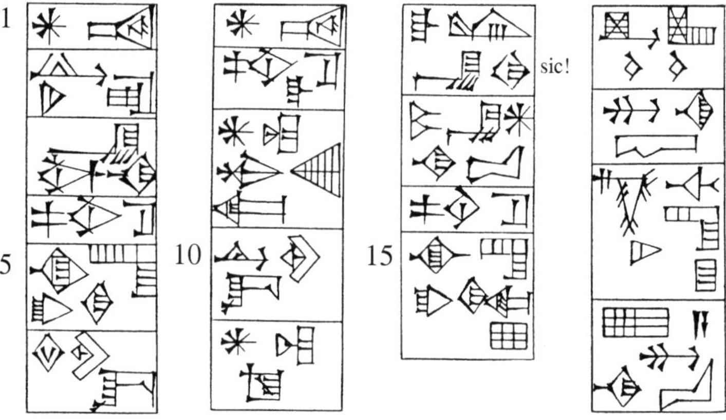

15

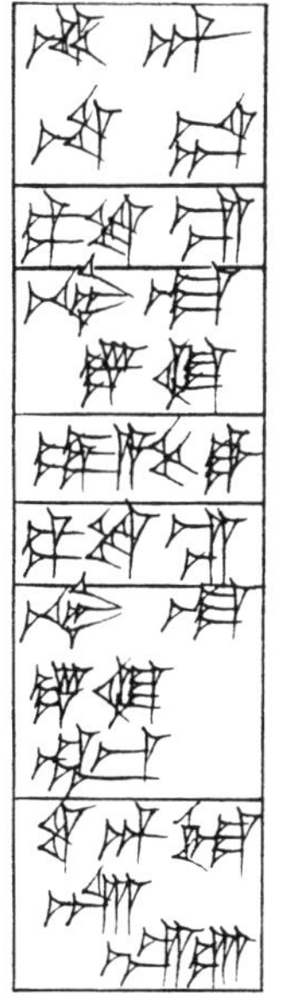

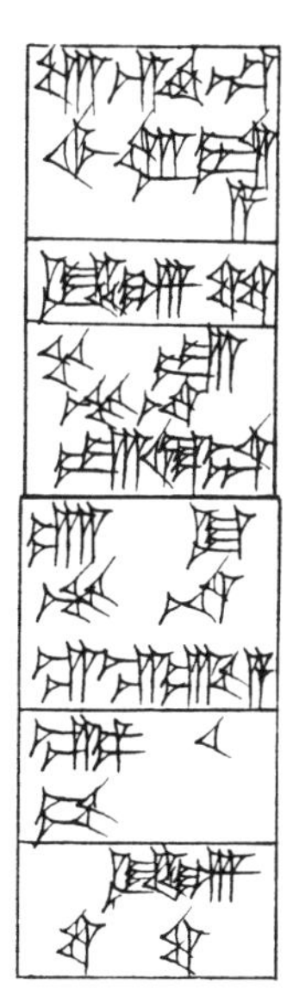

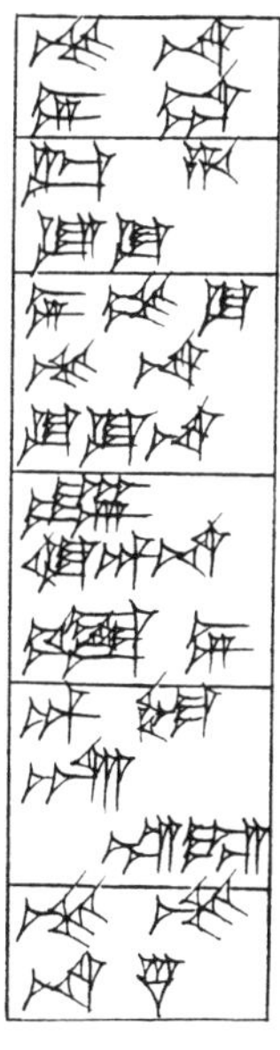

16

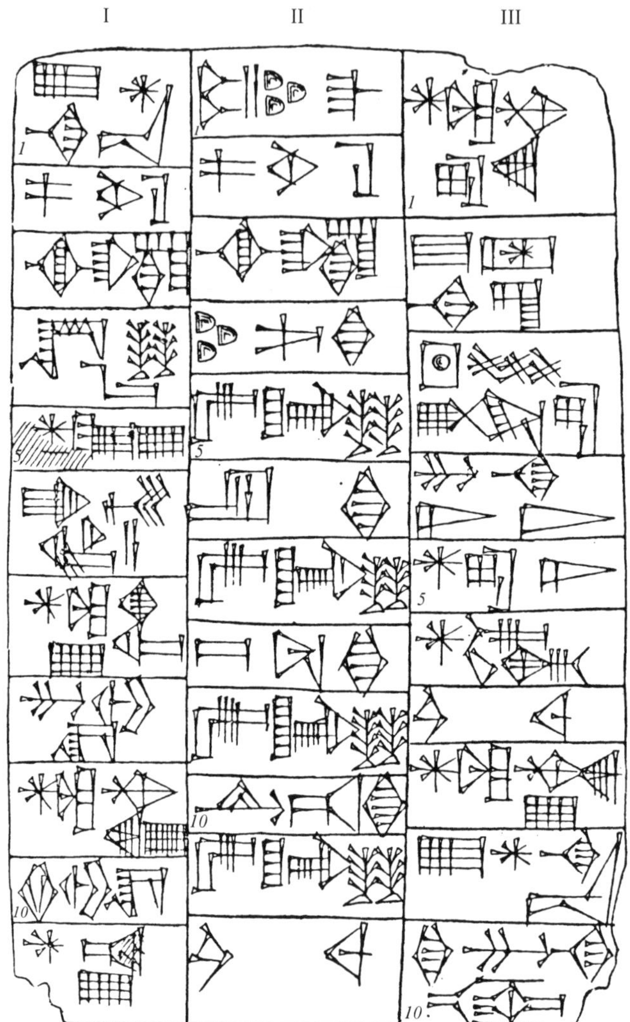

17

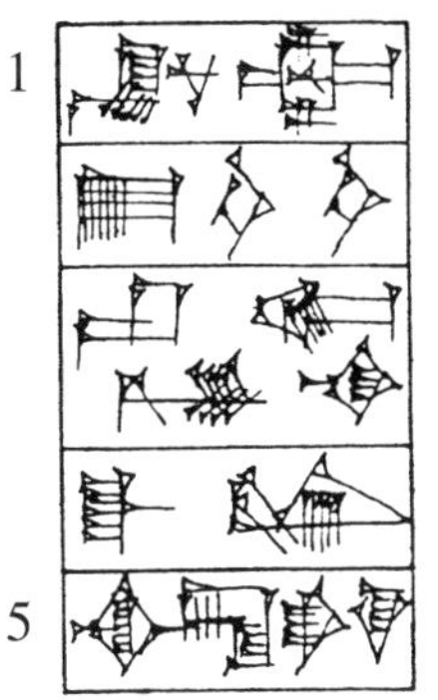

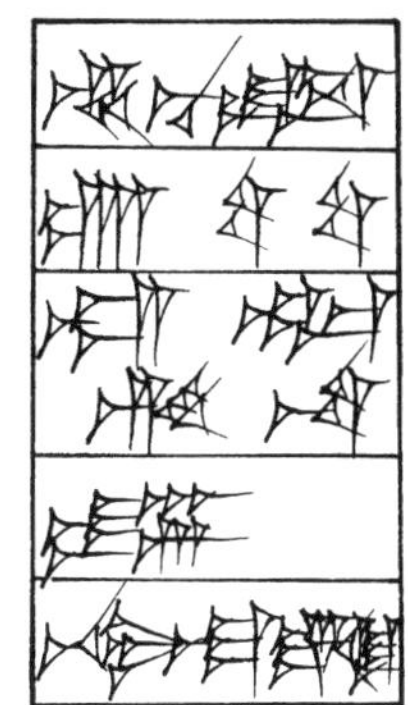

For the substantial variants of this type of inscription see H. Steible, FAOS 5/1, 338; FAOS 5/2, 170f.

18

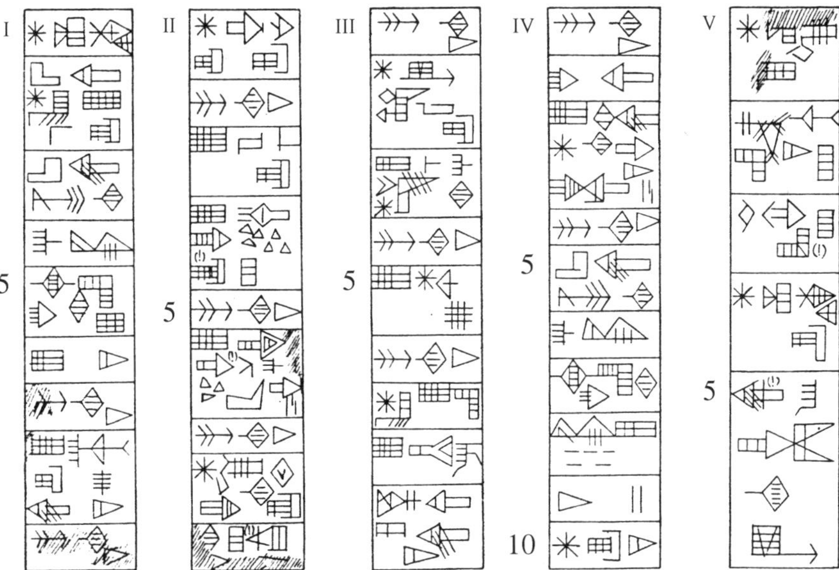

19

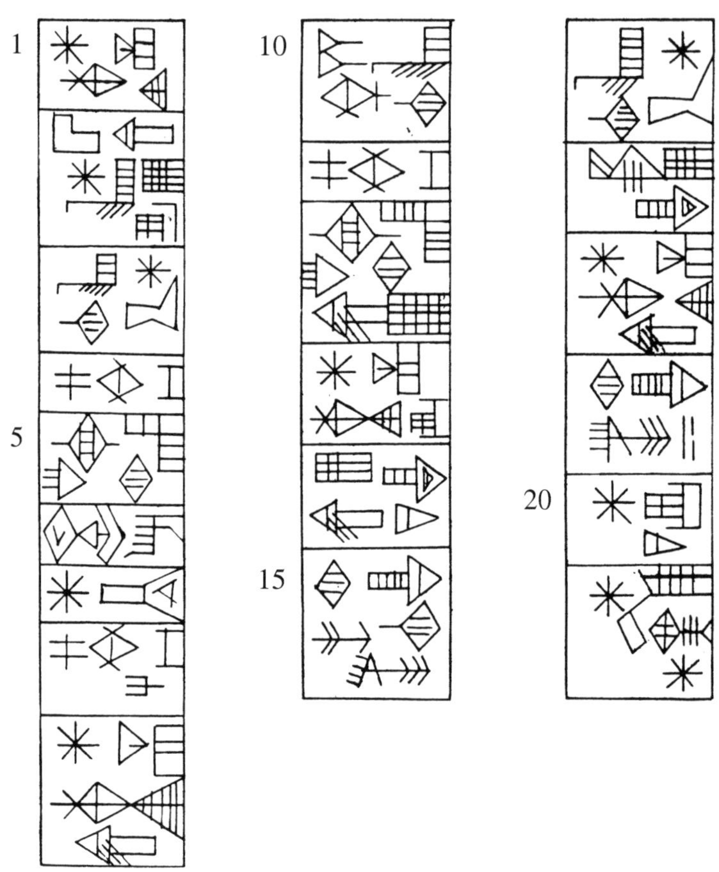

^{d}nin-ĝír-sú / ur-saĝ ^{d}en-líl-ra / en-an-na-túm / énsi(PA.TE.SI) / *(5)* lagas(NU$_{11}$.BUR.LA)^{ki} / šà pà-da / ^{d}našše / énsi-gal / ^{d}nin-ĝír-sú-ka / *(10)* dumu en-te:me-na / énsi(PA.TE.SI) / lagas(NU$_{11}$.BUR.LA)^{ki}-ka-ke$_4$ / ^{d}nin-ĝír-sú-ra / é-BI×NÍĜ-ka-ni / *(15)* ki-bé mu-na-ge$_4$ / en-an-na-túm / lú é-BI×NÍĜ / ^{d}nin-ĝír-sú-ka / ki-bé ge$_4$-a / *(20)* diĝir-ra-ni / ^{d}sul-luḫša-am$_6$

20

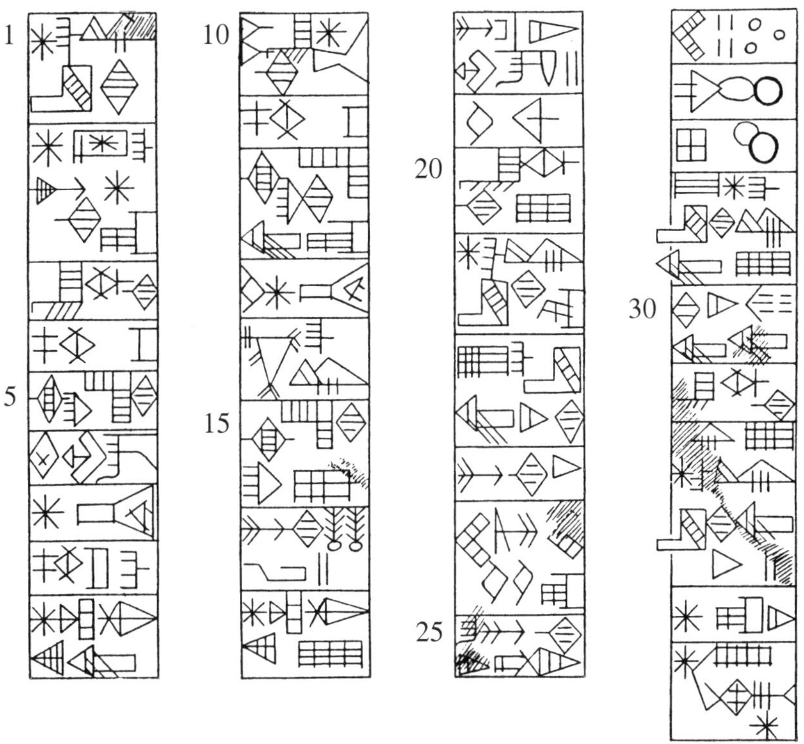

^{d}lugal-uru$_{11}$(URU×KÁR)^{ki} / ^{d}ama-ušumgal-an-na-ra / en-te:me-na / énsi(PA.TE.SI) / *(5)* lagas(NU$_{11}$.BUR.LA)^{ki} / šà pà-da / ^{d}našše / énsi(PA.TE.SI)-gal / ^{d}nin-g̃ír-sú-ka / *(10)* dumu en-an-na-túm / énsi (PA.TE.SI) / lagas(NU$_{11}$.BUR.LA)^{ki}-ka-ra$^{?!}$ / u$_{4}$ ^{d}našše / nam-lugal / *(15)* lagas(NU$_{11}$.BUR.LA)^{ki}-sa / mu-na-šúm-ma-a / ^{d}nin-g̃ír-sú-ke$_{4}$ / mu e-ni-pà-da-a / u$_{4}$-ba / *(20)* en-te:me-na-ke$_{4}$ / ^{d}lugal-uru$_{11}$(URU×KÁR)^{ki}-ra / é-gal uru$_{11}$(URU×KÁR)^{ki}-ka-ni / mu-na-dù / kù-si$_{22}$ ⸢kù⸣-bábbar-ra / *(25)* šu mu-na-ni-tà / kù za-gìn / gu$_{4}$ 20 / udu 20 / kisal ^{d}lugal-uru$_{11}$ (URU×KÁR)^{ki}-ka-ke$_{4}$ / *(30)* sá ì-mi-du$_{11}$-du$_{11}$ / en-te:me-na / [l]ú é ^{d}lugal-uru$_{11}$(URU×KÁR)^{ki}-ka dù-a / dig̃ir-ra-ni / ^{d}šul-luḫša-am$_{6}$

21

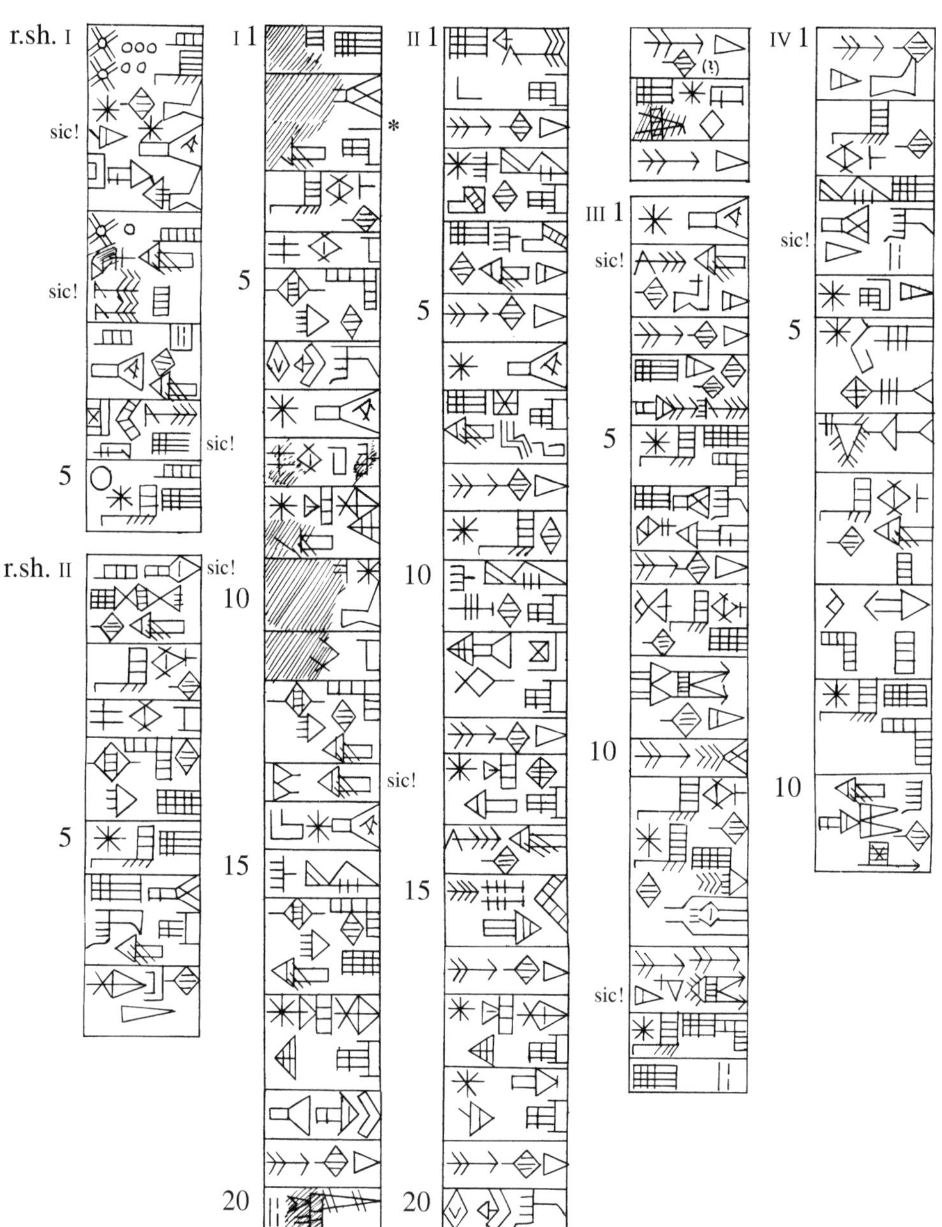

*This line is to be read [é]-ad-[da]-⸢ka⸣-ra, see r.sh. II 6.

22

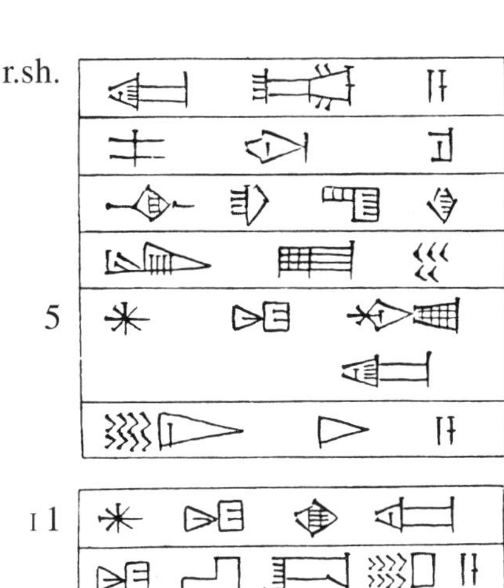

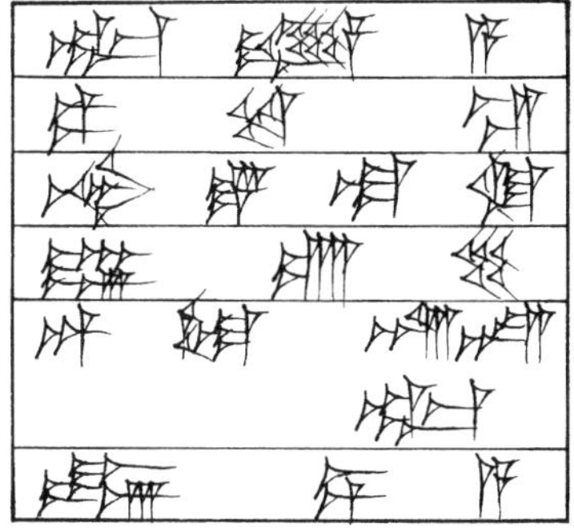

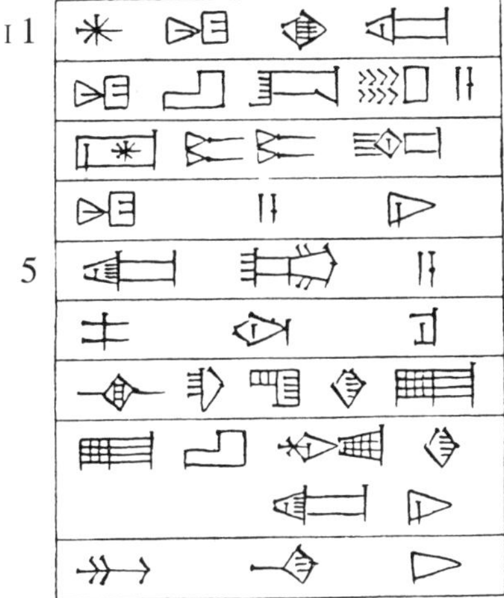

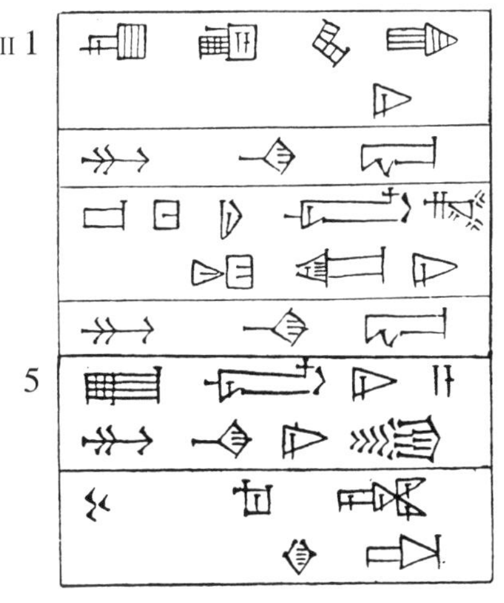

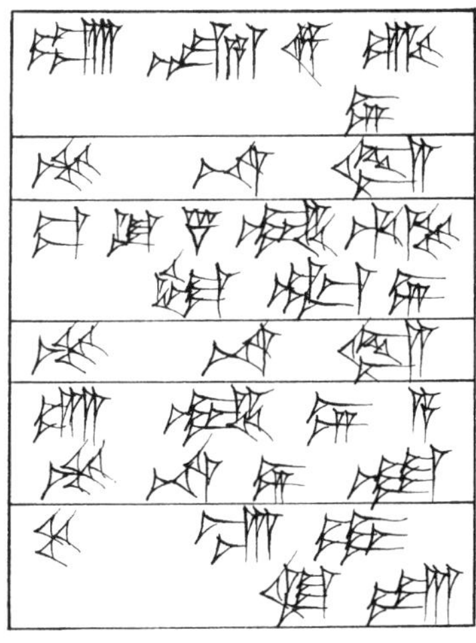

22 ctd.

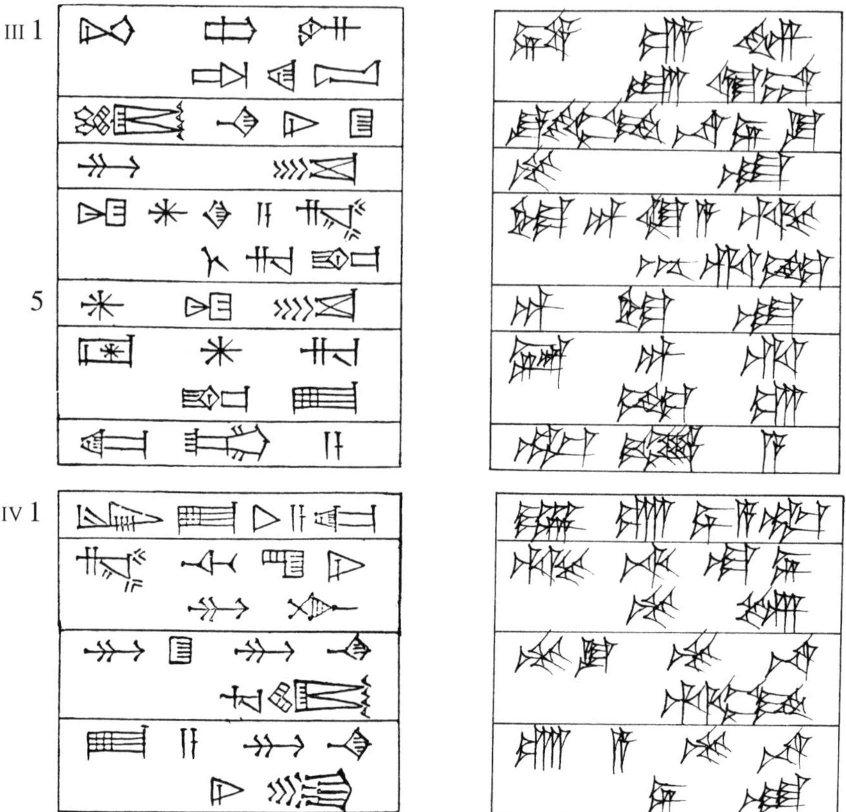

right shoulder gù-dé-a / énsi lagas^{ki} / lú é-ninnu / *(5)* ^{d}nin-ĝír-su-ka in-dù-a / (I) ^{d}nin-ḫur-saĝ / nin iri-da mú-a / ama dumu-dumu-ne / nin-a-ni / *(5)* gù-dé-a énsi / lagas^{ki}-ke$_4$ / é iri ĝír-su^{ki}-ka-ni / mu-na-dù / (II) dub-šen kù-ga-ni / mu-na-dím / ^{ĝeš}dúr-ĝar maḫ nam-nin-ka-ni / mu-na-dím / *(5)* é maḫ-ni-a mu-na-ni-ku$_4$ / kur má-gan^{ki}-ta / (III) ^{na_4}esi im-ta-e$_{11}$ alan-na-ni-šè / mu-dú / nin an ki-a nam-tar-re-dè / *(5)* ^{d}nin-tu / ama diĝir-re-ne-ke$_4$ / gù-dé-a / (IV) lú é dù-a-ka / nam-ti-la-ni mu-sù / mu-šè mu-na-še$_{21}$ / é-a mu-na-ni-ku$_4$

23

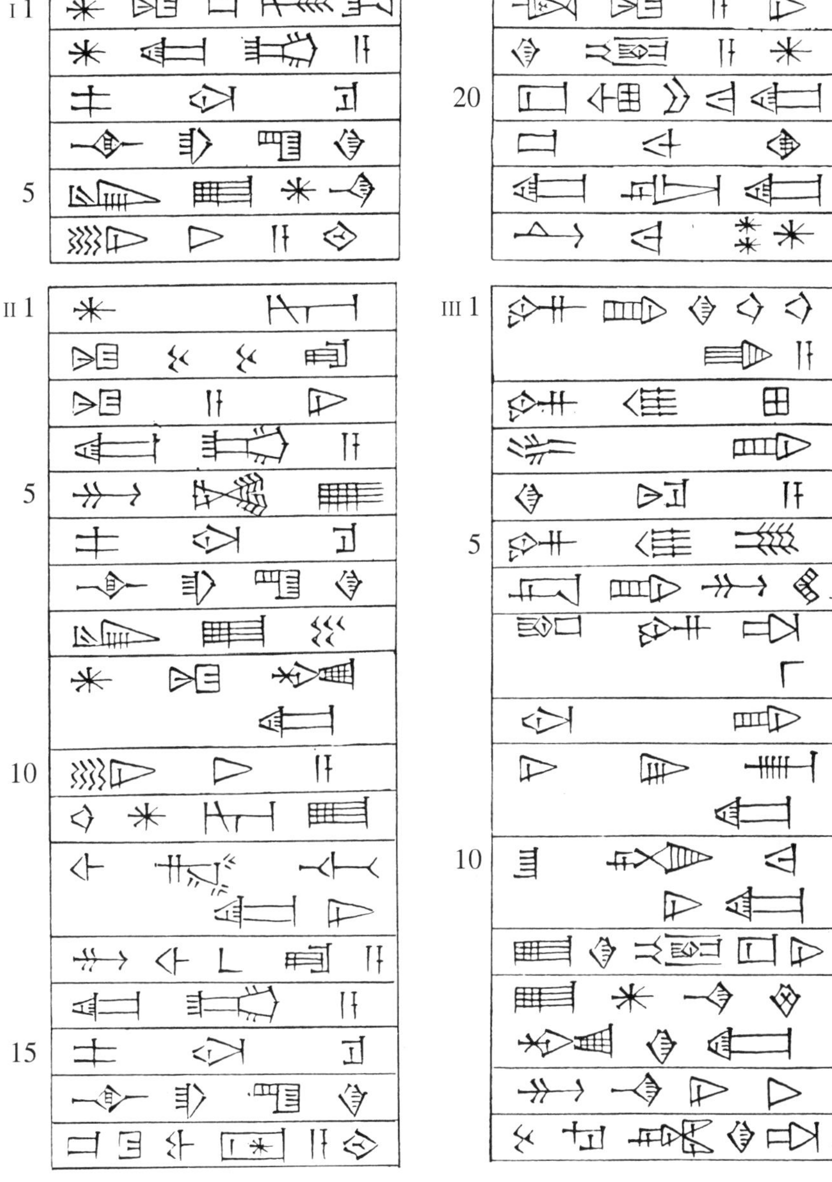

23 ctd.

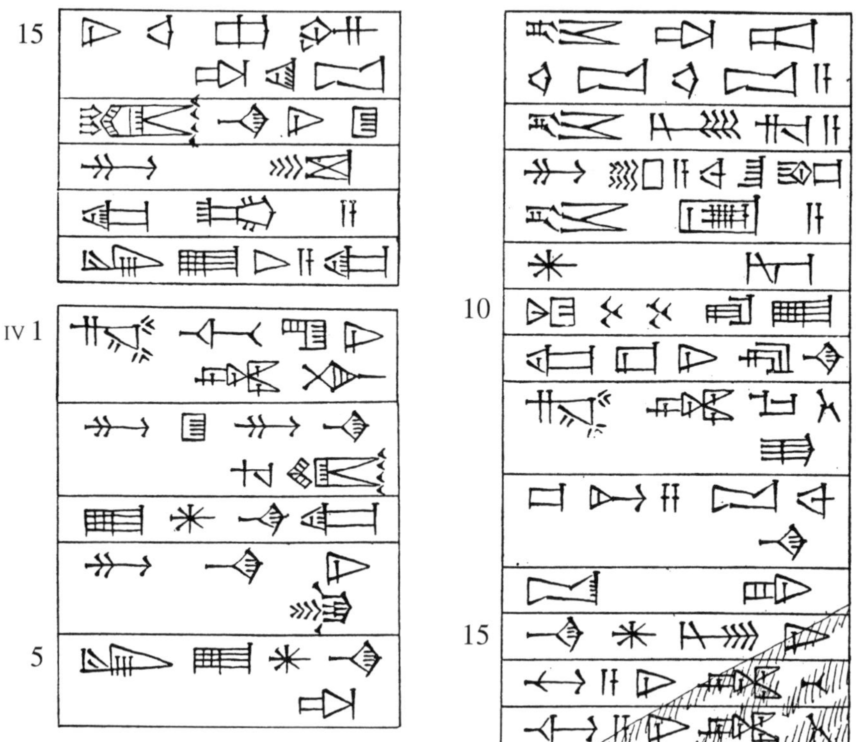

(I) ^{d}nin-ĝeš-zi-da / diĝir gù-dé-a / énsi / lagas^{ki} / *(5)* lú é-an-na / in-dù-a-kam / (II) ^{d}inana / nin kur-kur-ra / nin-a-ni / gù-dé-a *(5)* mu gi$_{16}$-sa / énsi / lagas^{ki} / lú é-ninnu / ^{d}nin-ĝír-su-ka / *(10)* in-dù-a / u$_{4}$ ^{d}inana-ke$_{4}$ / igi nam-ti-ka-ni / mu-ši-bar-ra-a / gù-dé-a / *(15)* énsi / lagas^{ki} / $^{ĝeš\text{-}tu_9}$ĝeštu daĝal-a-kam / úrdu nin-a-ni / ki-áĝ-àm / *(20)* ĝá ù-šub-ba-ka / ĝeš ba-ḫur / ka-al-ka / urin ba-mul / (III) im-bi ki dadag-ga-a / im-mi-lu / šeg$_{12}$-bi / ki sikil-a / *(5)* im-mi-du$_{8}$ / uš-bi mu-kù / izi im-ta-lá / temen-bi / ì ir nun-ka / *(10)* šu-tà ba-ni-du$_{11}$ / é ki-áĝ-ĝá-ni / é-an-na šà ĝír-su^{ki}-ka / mu-na-ni-dù / kur má-gan^{ki}-ta / *(15)* ^{na_4}esi im-ta-e$_{11}$ / alan-na-ni-šè / mu-dú / gù-dé-a / lú é dù-a-ka / (IV) nam-ti-la-ni ḫé-sù / mu-šè mu-na-še$_{21}$ / é-an-na-ka / mu-na-ni-ku$_{4}$ / *(5)* lú é-an-na-ta / íb-ta-ab-è-è-a / íb-zi-re-a / mu-sar-a-ba šu bí-íb-uru$_{12}$-a / ^{d}inana / *(10)* nin kur-kur-ra-ke$_{4}$ / saĝ-ĝá-ni unken-na / nam ḫé-ma-ku$_{5}$-e / ^{ĝeš}gu-za gub-ba-na / suḫuš-bi / *(15)* na-an-gi-⸢né⸣ / nuĝun-a-ni ⸢ḫé-til⸣ / bala-⸢a-ni ḫé-ku$_{5}$⸣

24

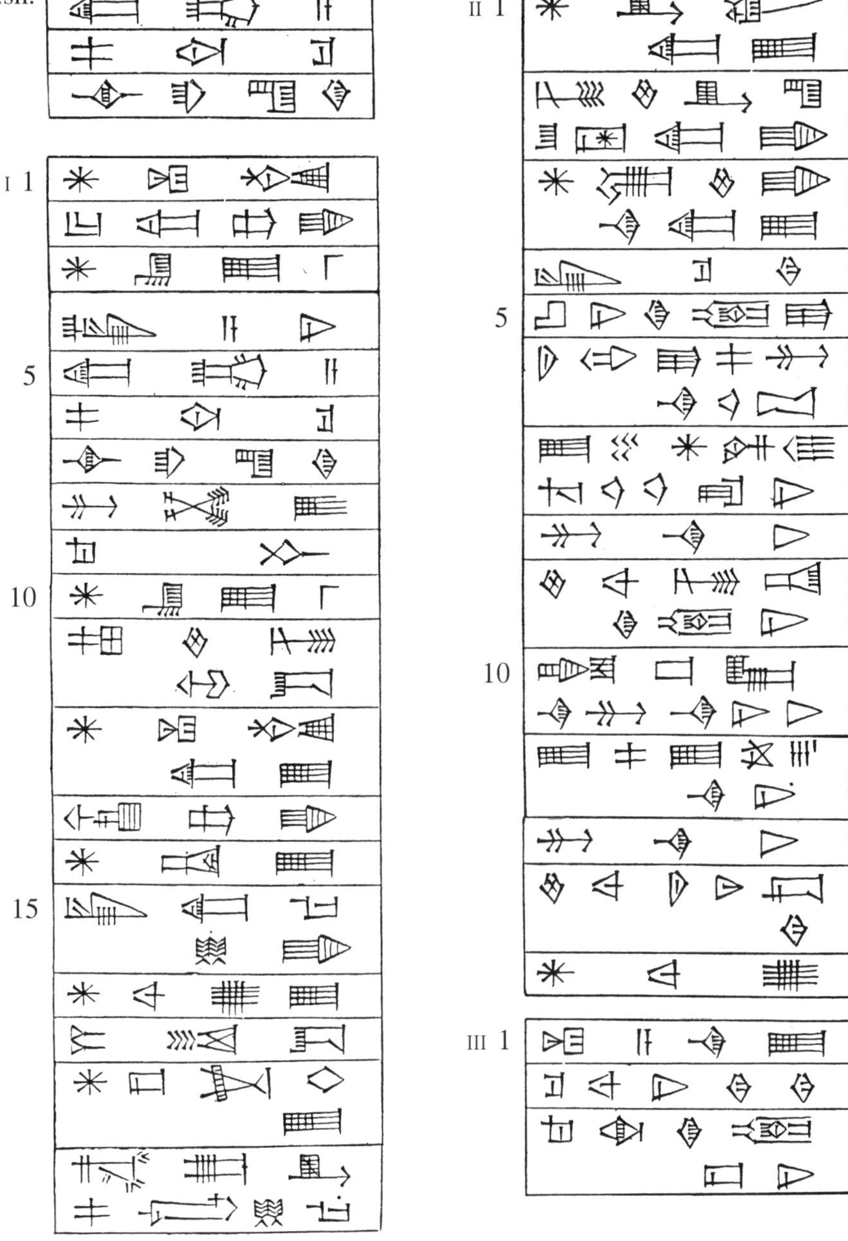

24 ctd.

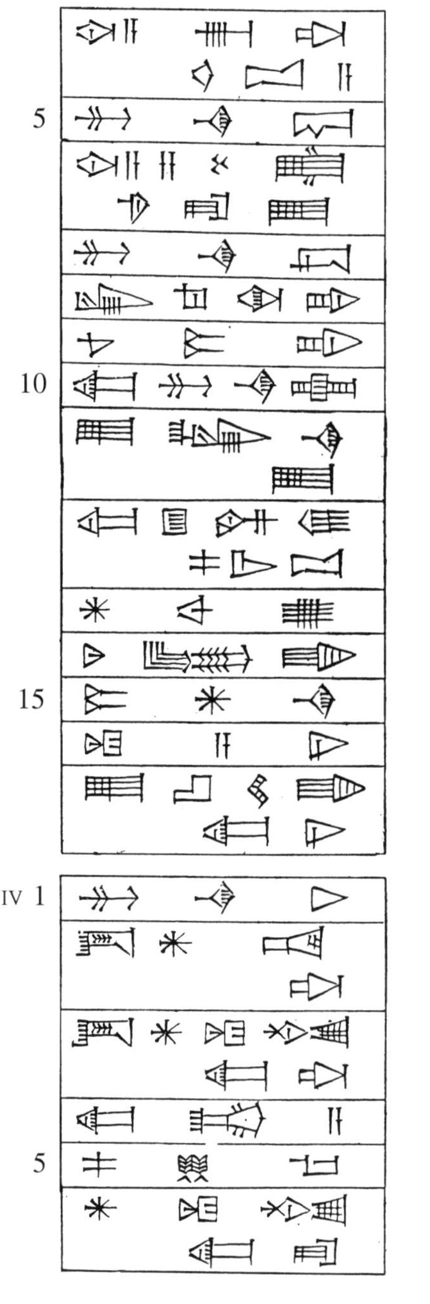

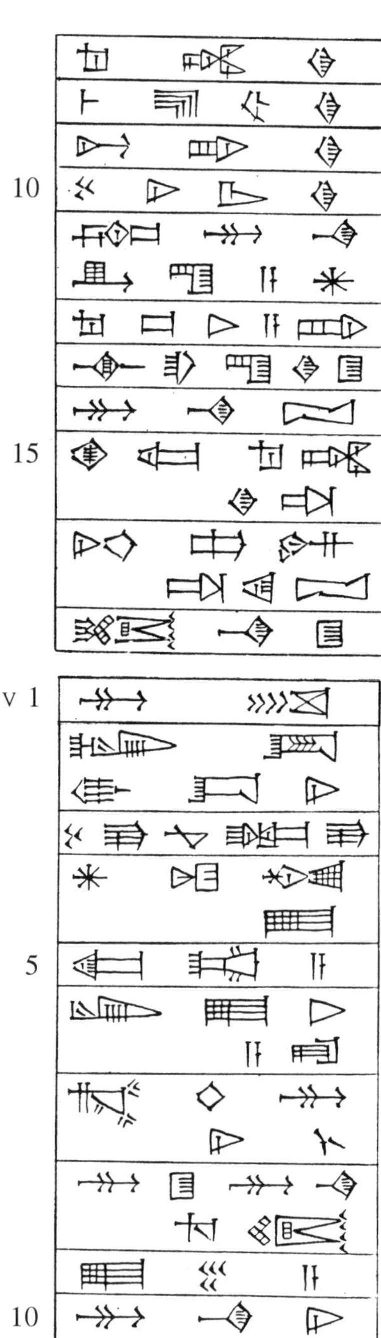

25

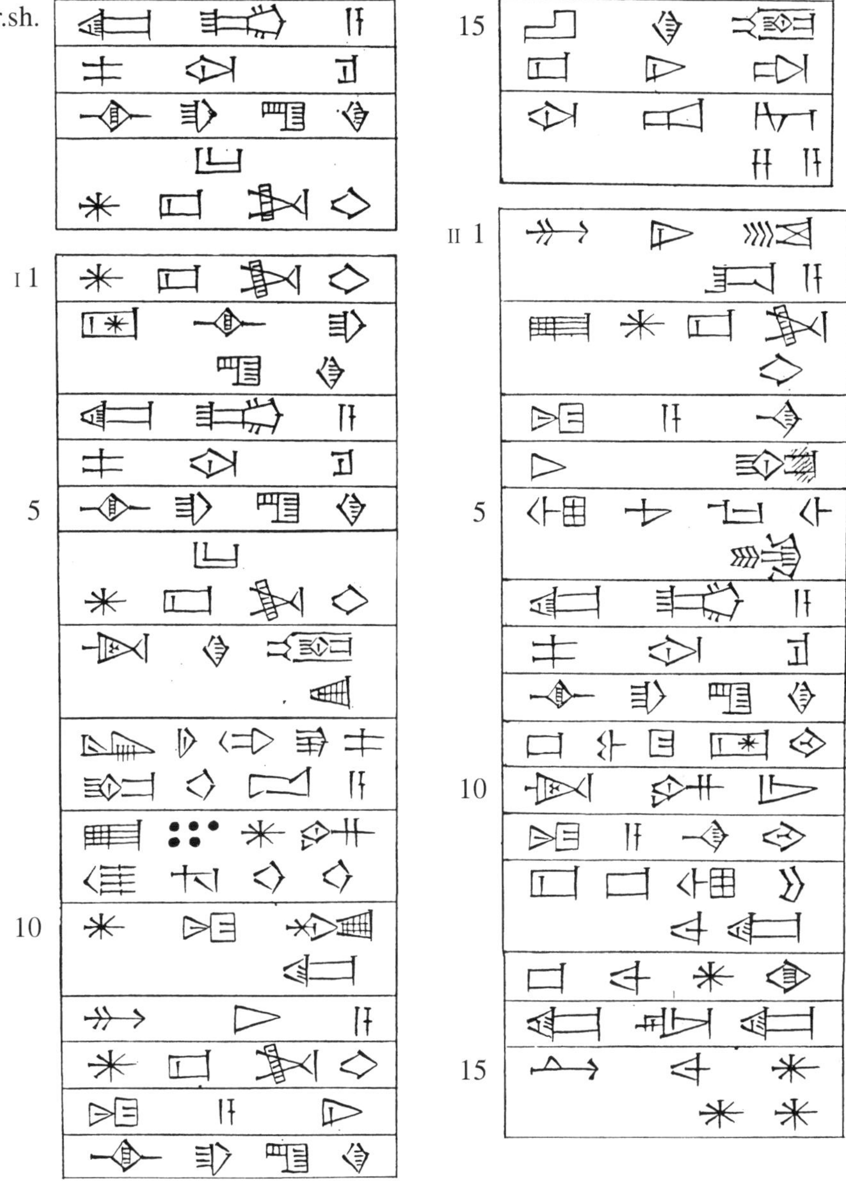

25 ctd.

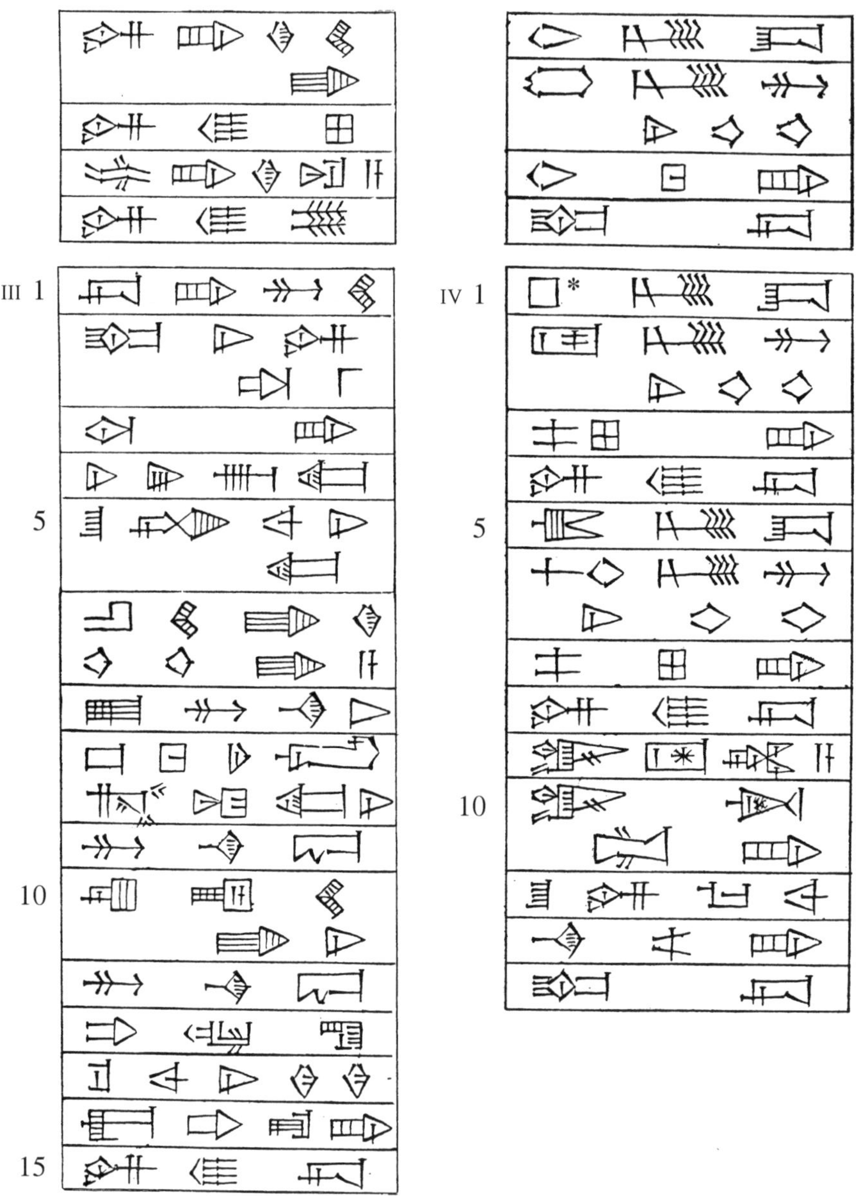

* Collation shows a clear

26

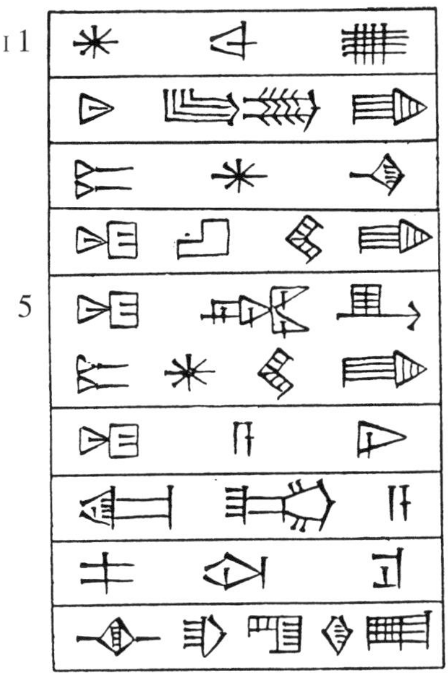

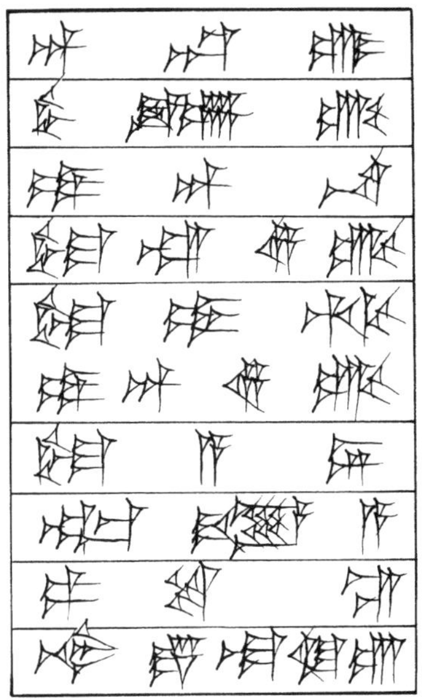

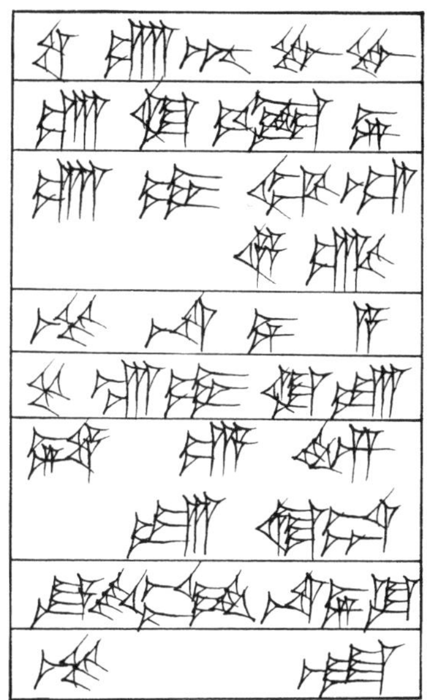

26 ctd.

III 1

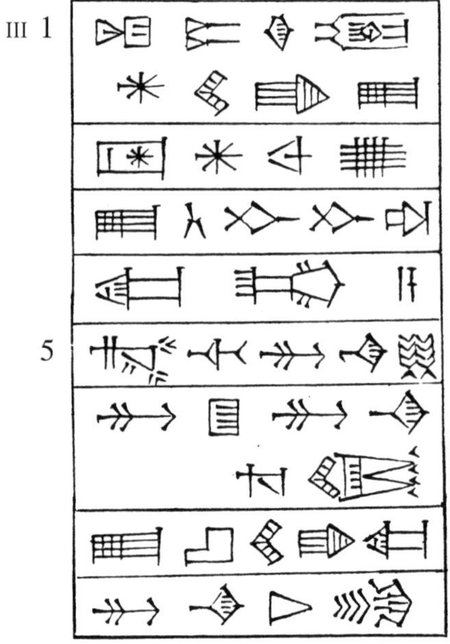

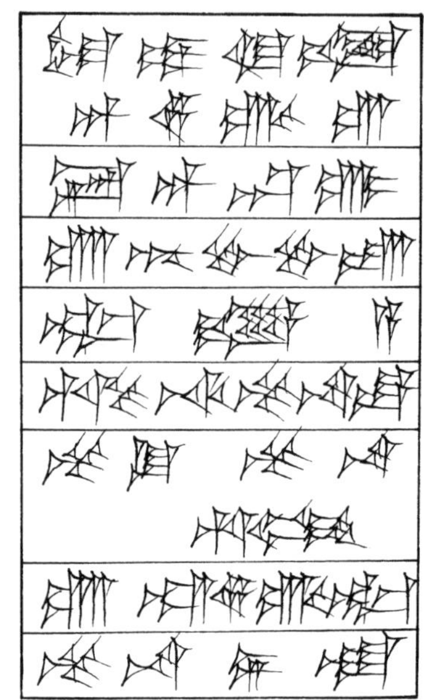

(I) ^{d}ba-Ú / munus sa$_{6}$-ga / dumu an-na / nin iri-kù-ga / *(5)* nin ḫ̮é-g̃ál dumu an kù-ga / nin-a-ni / gù-dé-a / énsi / lagas^{ki}-ke$_{4}$ /

(II) u$_{4}$ é-tar-sír-sír / é ki-ág̃-ni / é ḫ̮é-du$_{7}$ iri-kù-ga / mu-na-dù-a / *(5)* kur má-gan^{ki}-ta / ^{na_4}esi$^{!}$(=PA) im-ta-e$_{11}$ / alan-na-ni-šè / mu-dú

(III) nin dumu ki-ág̃ an kù-ga-ke$_{4}$ / ama ^{d}ba-Ú / é-tar-sír-sír-ta / gù-dé-a / *(5)* nam-ti mu-na-šúm / mu-šè mu-na-še$_{21}$ / é iri-kù-ga-ka / mu-na-ni$^{!}$(=GAG)-ku$_{4}$

27

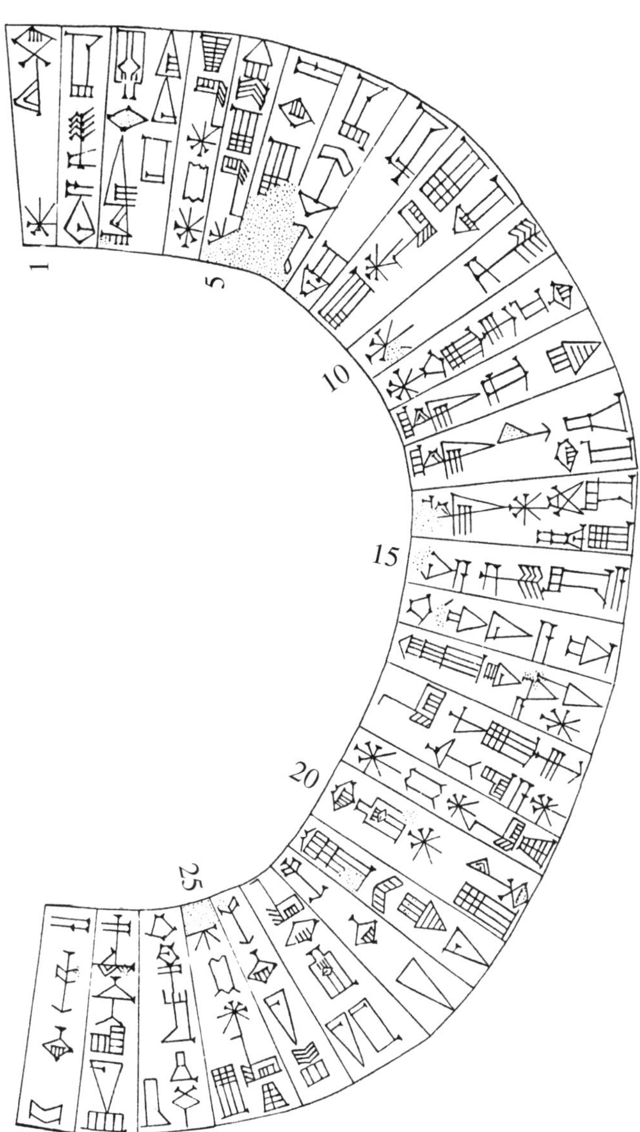

^{d}nanna
kar-zi-da
lugal ⸢ki⸣-áĝ-ĝá-ni-ir
^{d}amar-^{d}*zuen*
⸢^{d}⸣en-líl-le
[nib]ru^{ki}-a
⸢mu⸣ pà-da
saĝ-ús
é ^{d}en-líl-ka
diĝir zi
^{d}utu kalam-ma-na
lugal kala-ga
lugal uri$_{5}$^{ki}-ma
[l]ugal an-ub-da
límmu-ba-ke$_{4}$
kar-zi-da-a
u$_{4}$ ul-lí-a-ta
ĝe$_{6}$-par$_{4}$-bi nu$^{!}$-dù-àm
en nu-un-ti-la-àm
^{d}amar-^{d}*zuen*
ki-áĝ ^{d}nanna-ke$_{4}$
ĝe$_{6}$-par$_{4}$ kù-ga-ni
mu-na-dù
en ki-áĝ-ĝá-ni
mu-na-ni-ku$_{4}$
⸢^{d}⸣amar-^{d}*zuen*-ke$_{4}$
u$_{4}$ im-da-ab-su$_{13}$-re$_{6}$
nam-ti-la-ni-šè
a mu-na-ru

28

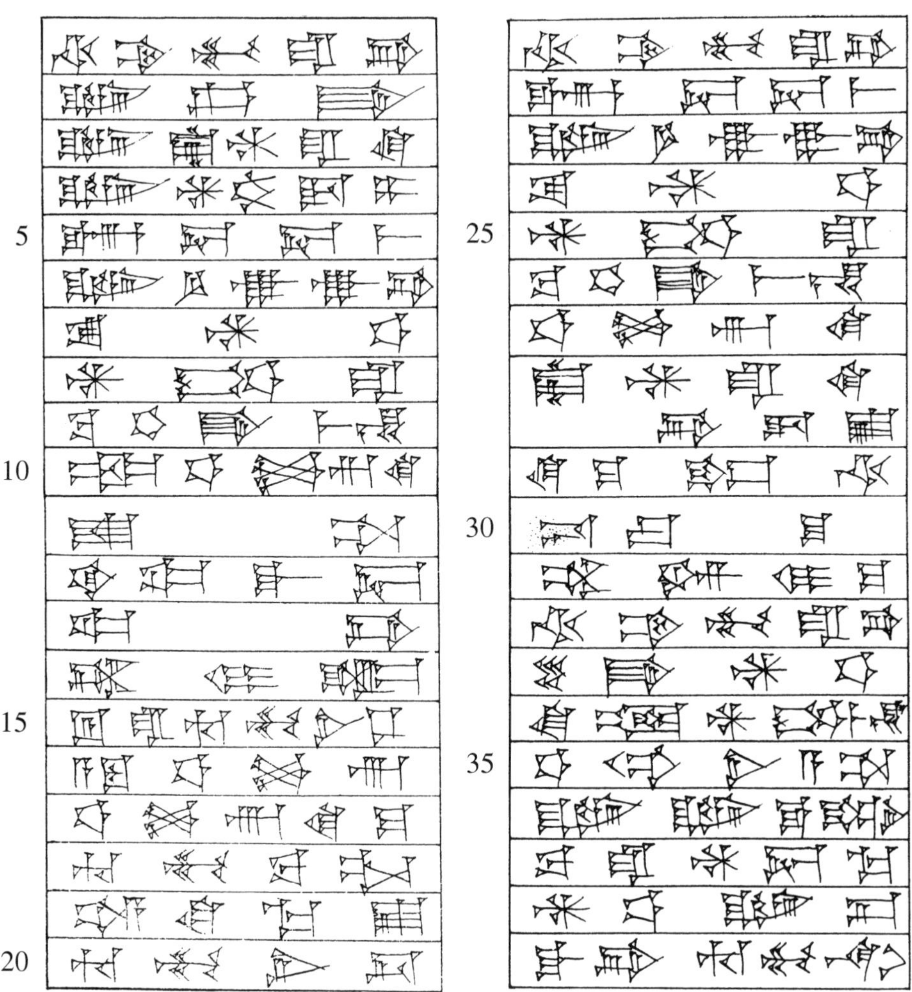

This is the Sumerian part of a bilingual text, and should be read in light of the Akkadian original. See the List of Texts, p. XVIII, 28.

29

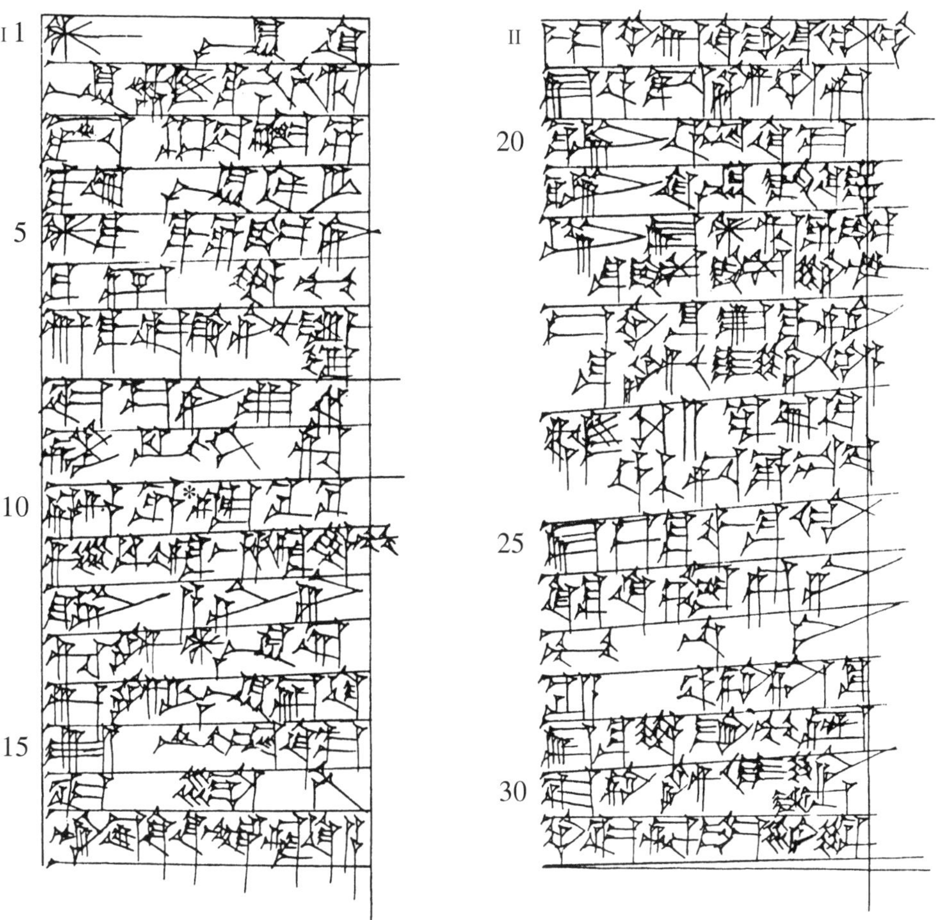

*According to a recent collation by I.L. Finkel the sign in question looks as follows:

30

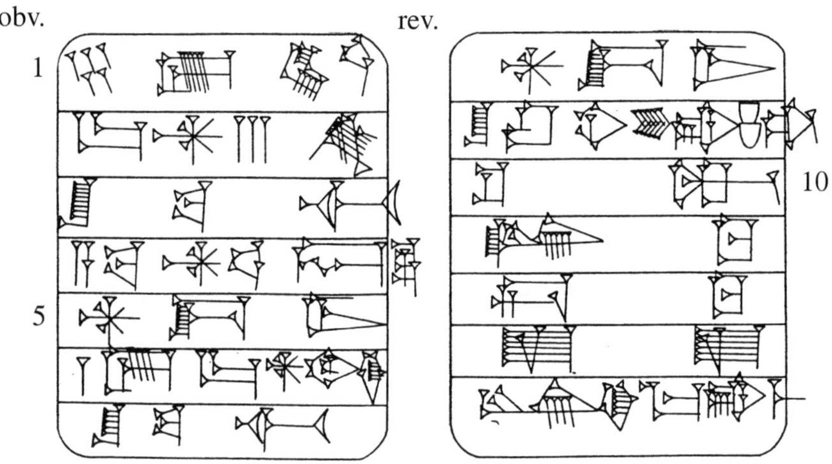

obv. 5 gĩg$_4$ kù-babbar
ur-^{d}eš$_5$-peš
šu ba-ti
a-ba-^{d}utu-gen$_7$-e
an-da-tuku
1 gĩg$_4$ ur-kèš^{ki}
šu ba-ti
rev. an-da-tuku
šu-rí-kam še-bi 2(bariga)-ta
si-dam
lugal-KU
gala
IŠ kuš$_7$
lú ki-<inim->ma-bi-me

31

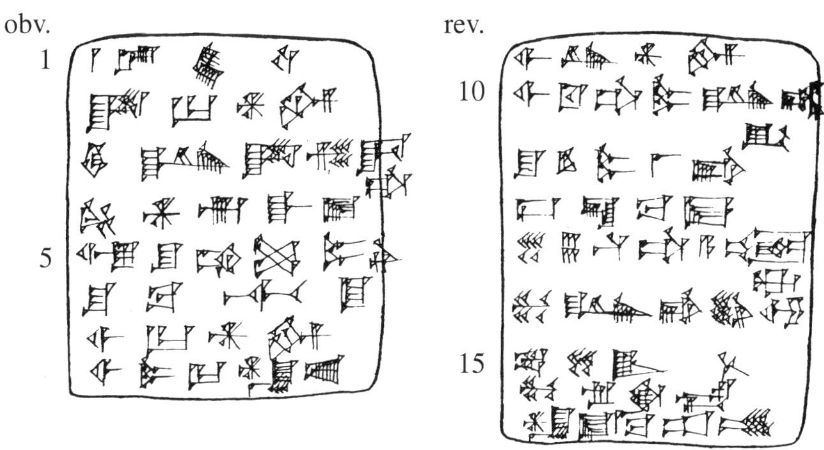

obv. 1 gig̃$_4$ kù-babbar
á ur-^{d}iškur
ki lugal-á-zi-da-ta
géme-^{d}nun-gal-ke$_4$
ù *šu-duran*(DUR$^{!}$.KIB) dumu-ni
šu ba-ti-éš
igi ur-^{d}iškur
igi dumu ur-^{d}*zuen*
rev. igi lú-^{d}iškur
igi pú-ta dumu lugal-ḫé-g̃ál
tukum-bi
g̃á-la ba-dag
še 6 sìla-ta a-ág̃-dam
mu lugal-bi in-pà
iti še-saga$_{11}$-ku$_5$
mu má-gur$_8$ maḫ
^{d}en-líl-lá ba-ab-du$_8$

32

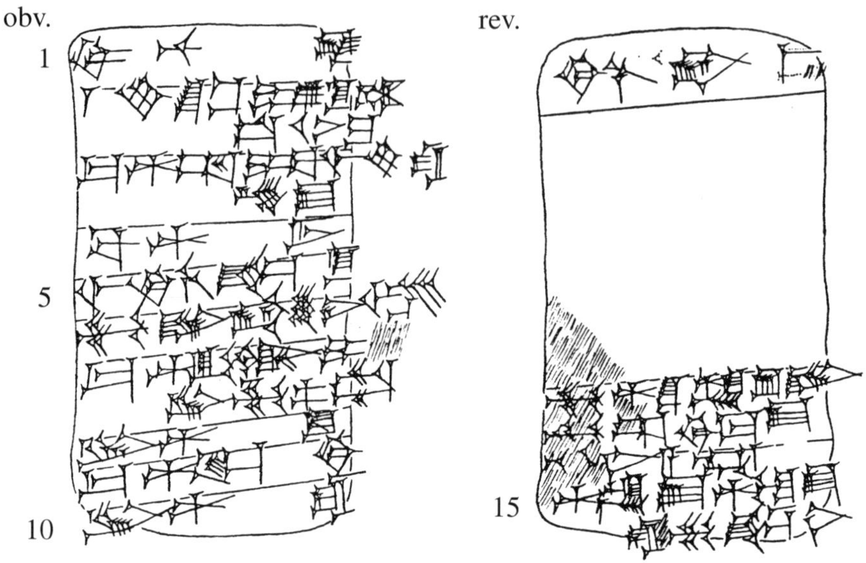

obv. di-til-la
^{I}šà-šu-níĝen dumu ú-šè-ḫ̮é-DU ùnu
ur-^{d}našše dumu ba-ši-šà-ra-ge-ke$_4$
ba-an-tuku
igi di-ku$_5$-ne-šè
mu lugal-bi in-pà-eš
ur-^{d}ig-alim dumu lú-ĝu$_{10}$ maškim
lú-^{d}šára
ur-^{d}ištaran
lú-diĝir-ra
rev. di-ku$_5$-bi-me
(space)
mu ^{d}*šu*-^{d}*sîn* lugal
uri$_5$^{ki}-ma-ke$_4$
na-rú-a maḫ̮
^{d}en-líl ^{d}nin-líl-ra mu-ne-dù

33

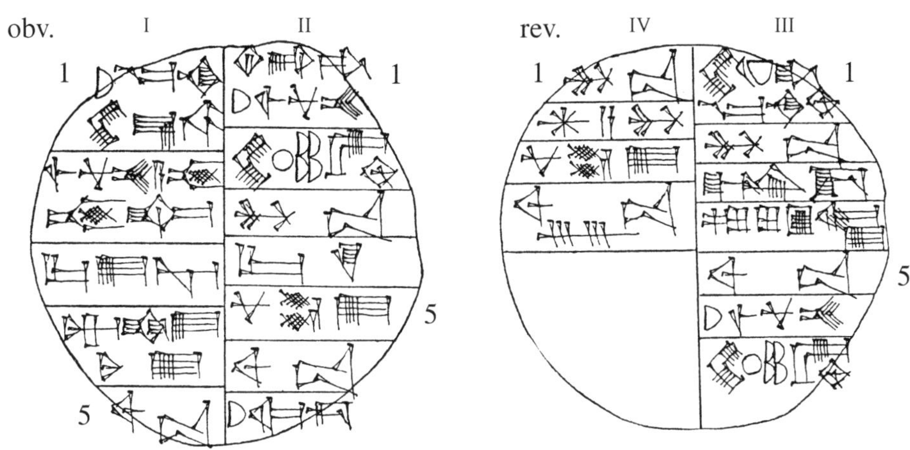

34

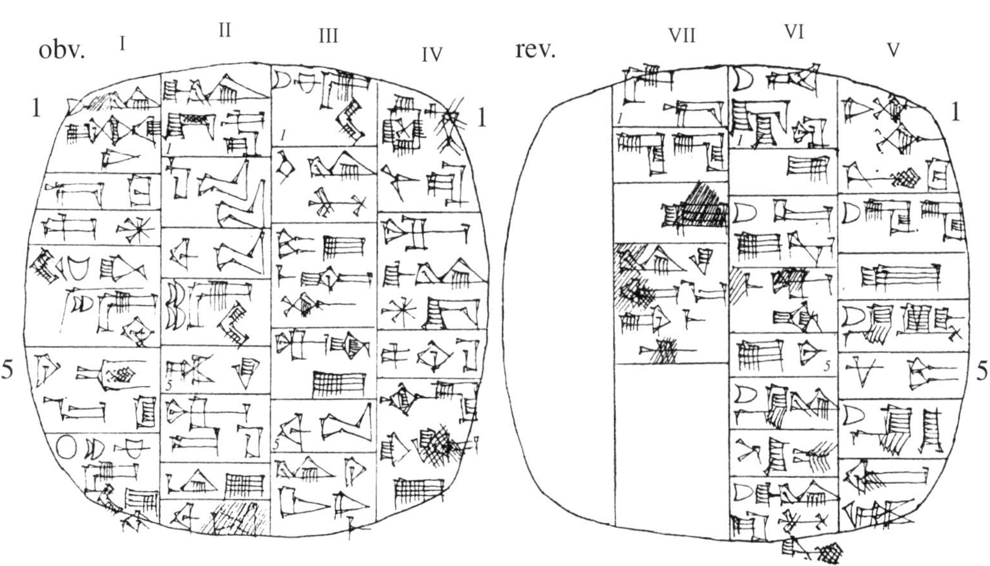

35

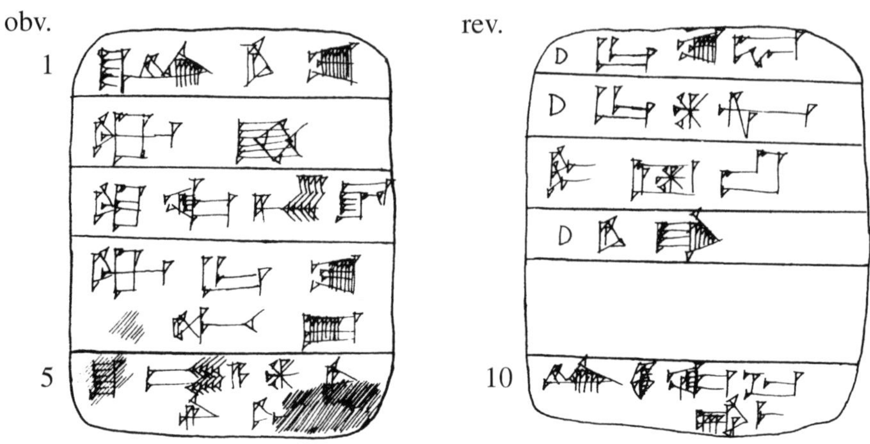

obv. lugal-níĝ-zu
dam-gàra
nin-inim-zi-da
dam ur-su nagar-ke$_4$
šu-du$_8$-a-an-ni* ì-⸢de$_6$⸣
rev. ^{I}ur-su$^{!}$ šidim
^{I}ur-^{d}inana
dumu ama-iri
^{I}níĝ-gur$_{11}$
(space)
lú ki-inim-ma-bi-me

*For this rare variant of /-a-ni/ in the Ur III-period see ÉLS § 108 a) *3e sg. p.*

36

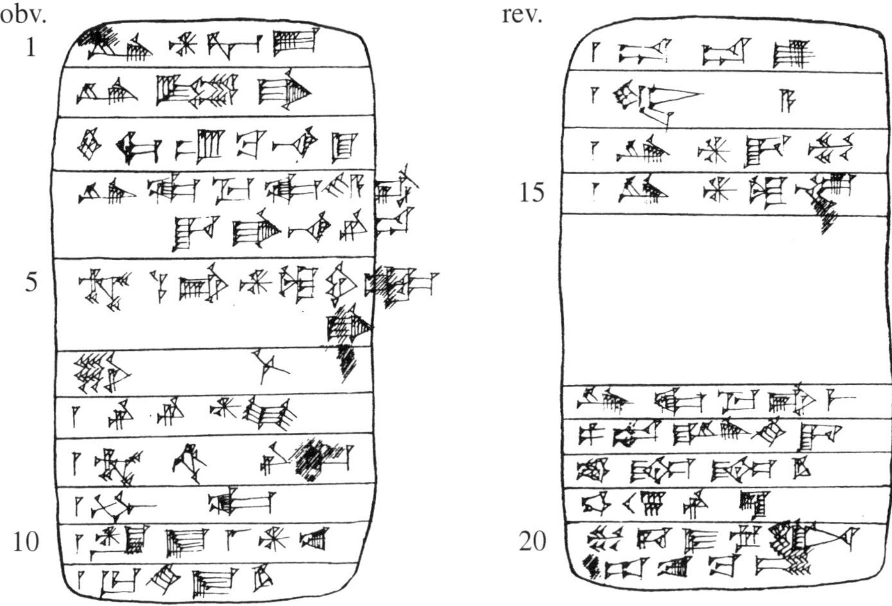

37

obv.

rev.

38

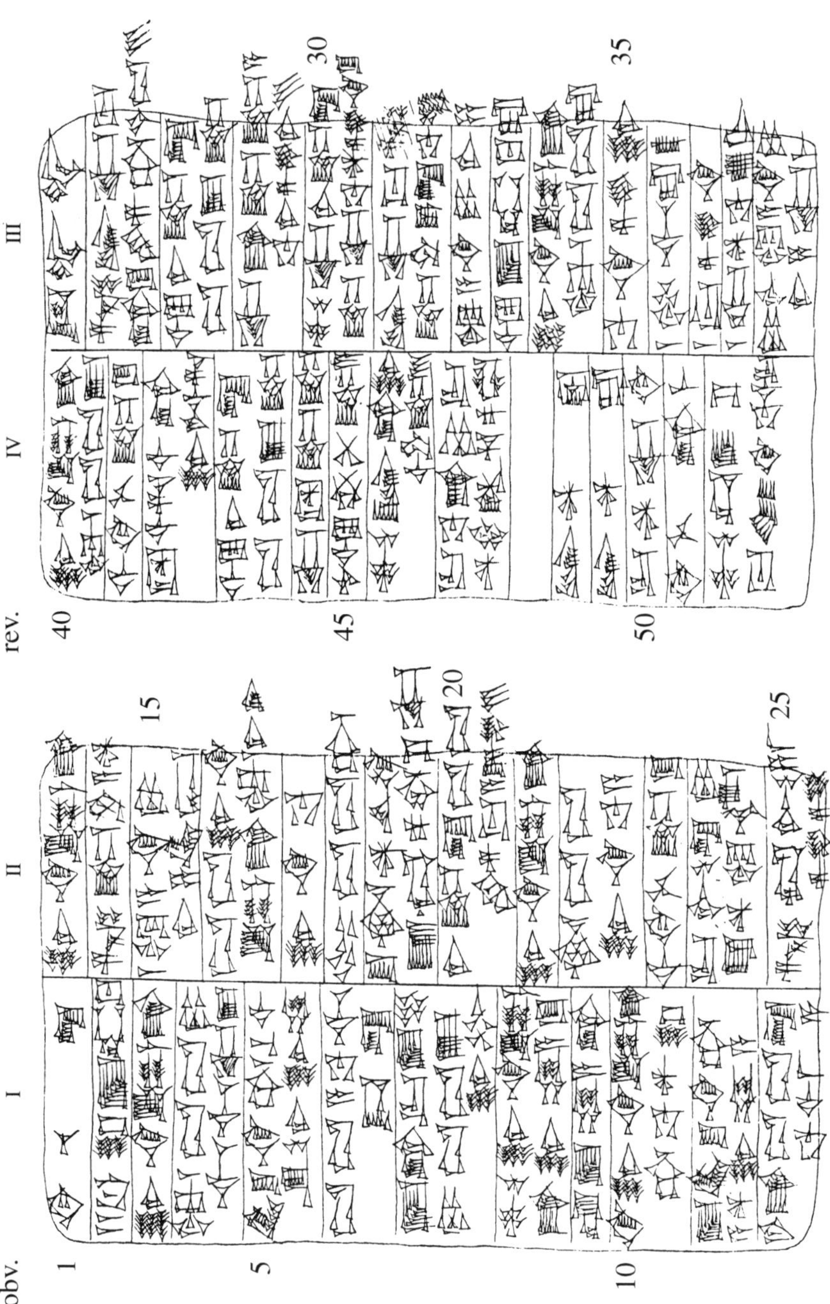

39

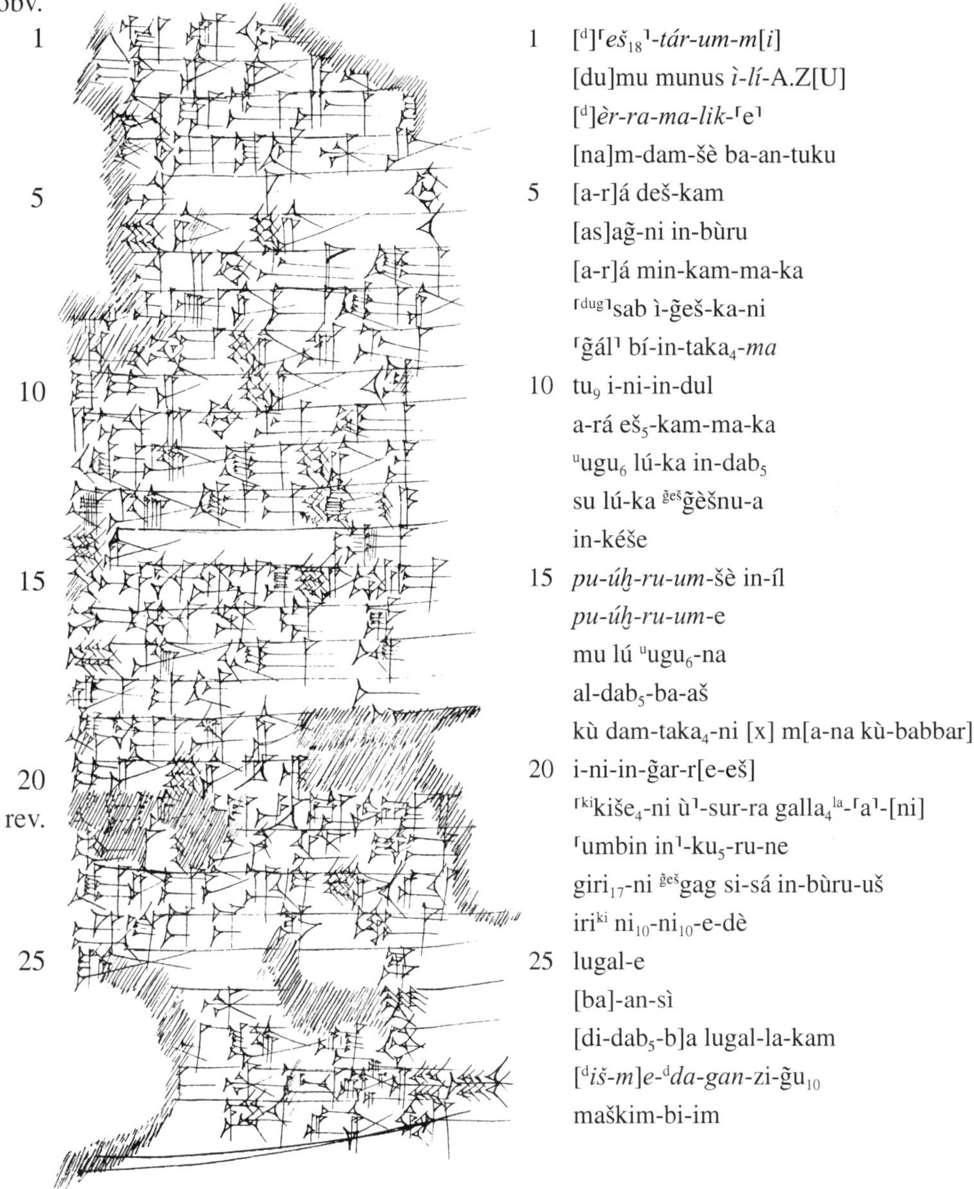

obv.

[^{d}]⸢*eš*$_{18}$⸣-*tár-um-m*[*i*]
[du]mu munus *ì-lí*-A.Z[U]
[^{d}]*èr-ra-ma-lik*-⸢e⸣
[na]m-dam-šè ba-an-tuku
[a-r]á deš-kam
[as]ag̃-ni in-bùru
[a-r]á min-kam-ma-ka
⸢^{dug}⸣sab ì-g̃eš-ka-ni
⸢g̃ál⸣ bí-in-taka$_4$-*ma*
tu$_9$ i-ni-in-dul
a-rá eš$_5$-kam-ma-ka
^{u}ugu$_6$ lú-ka in-dab$_5$
su lú-ka $^{\text{g̃eš}}$g̃èšnu-a
in-kéše
pu-úḫ-ru-um-šè in-íl
pu-úḫ-ru-um-e
mu lú ^{u}ugu$_6$-na
al-dab$_5$-ba-aš
kù dam-taka$_4$-ni [x] m[a-na kù-babbar]
i-ni-in-g̃ar-r[e-eš]

rev.

⸢^{ki}kiše$_4$-ni ù⸣-sur-ra galla$_4$^{la}-⸢a⸣-[ni]
⸢umbin in⸣-ku$_5$-ru-ne
giri$_{17}$-ni $^{\text{g̃eš}}$gag si-sá in-bùru-uš
iri^{ki} ni$_{10}$-ni$_{10}$-e-dè
lugal-e
[ba]-an-sì
[di-dab$_5$-b]a lugal-la-kam
[^{d}*iš-m*]*e*-^{d}*da-gan*-zi-g̃u$_{10}$
maškim-bi-im

The interpretation of the faint traces at the beginning of line 21 as ⸢^{ki}kiše$_4$⸣ is highly tentative, though persuasive. Accordingly, the sign kiše$_4$ has not been included in the Sign List, and the reader is referred to the information given on p. XVIII, 39.

40

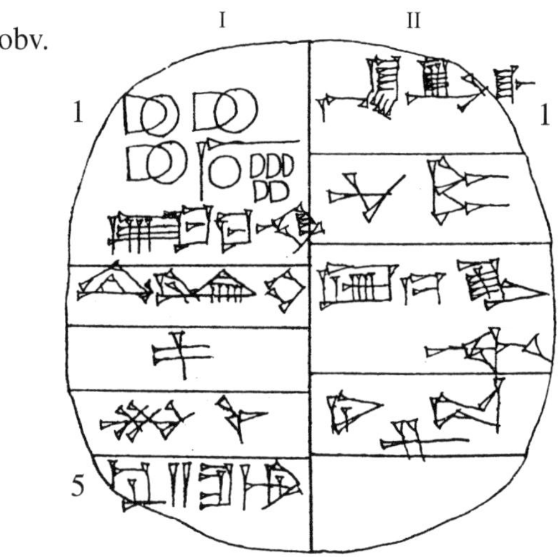

reverse blank

obv. I 1800 lá 15 sa <ú->durun$_{x}$-na
ses-lú-du$_{10}$
ugula
mu-ku$_{5}$
má-a$^{!}$ e-me-g̃ar

obv. II en-ig-gal
nu-bànda
g̃anun g̃eš-kíg̃-ti
ì-de$_{6}$ 2

41

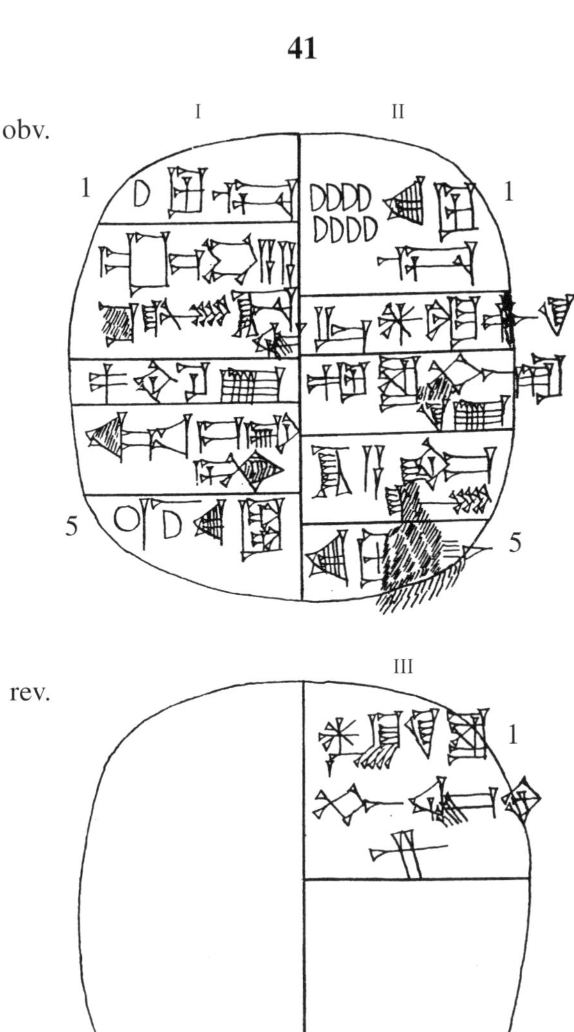

(I) 1 udu-ninta / izim amar-a-a-⸢si⸣-ge$_4$-da-ka / énsi-ke$_4$ / ⸢abzu⸣ g̃eš bé-tag / *(5)* 10 lá 1 kuš u$_8$ / (II) 8 kuš udu-ninta / ur-^{d}nin-MAR.KI / sipa pa$_5$-sír-ra^{ki}-ke$_4$ / šu-a bí-gi$_4$ / *(5)* kuš ud[u] ⸢ú⸣-rum / (III) ^{d}en-ki pa$_5$-sír-ka-kam 2

42

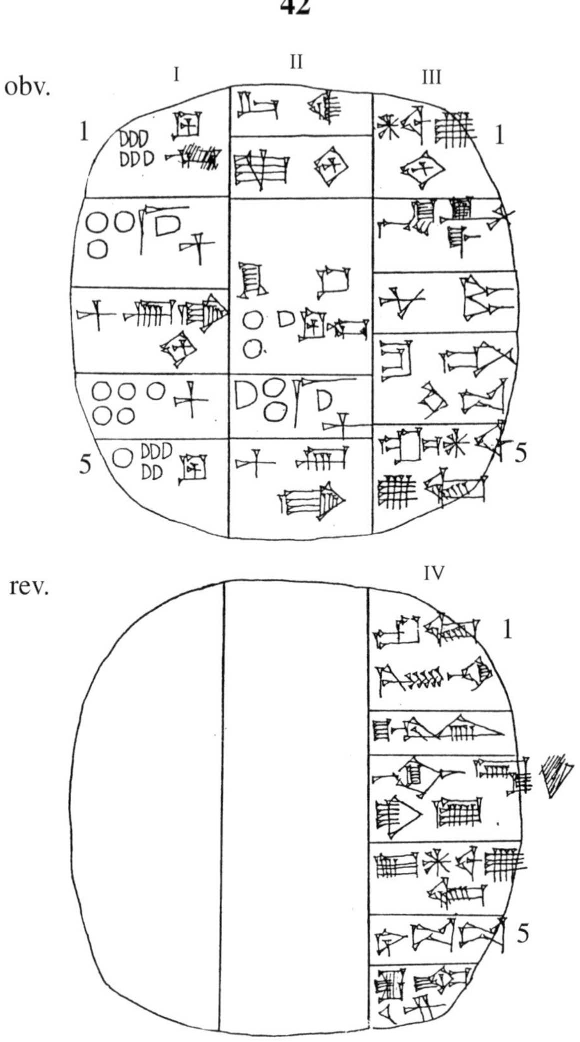

(I) 6 udu-⌜ninta⌝ / 30 lá 1 maš / maš aša$_{5}$-ga-kam / 50 maš / *(5)* 15 udu / (II) ur-du$_{6}$ / kuš$_{7}$-kam / šu-níĝen 21 udu-ninta / 80 lá 1 maš / *(5)* maš aša$_{5}$-ga / (III) ^{d}ba-Ú-kam / en-ig-gal / nu-bànda / e-ta-è / *(5)* izim ^{d}ba-Ú-ka (IV) iri-KA-gi-na / lugal / lagas$^{\ulcorner ki \urcorner}$-ke$_{4}$ / é ^{d}ba-Ú-ka / *(5)* ì-laḫ$_{5}$ / zà bí-šuš 2

43

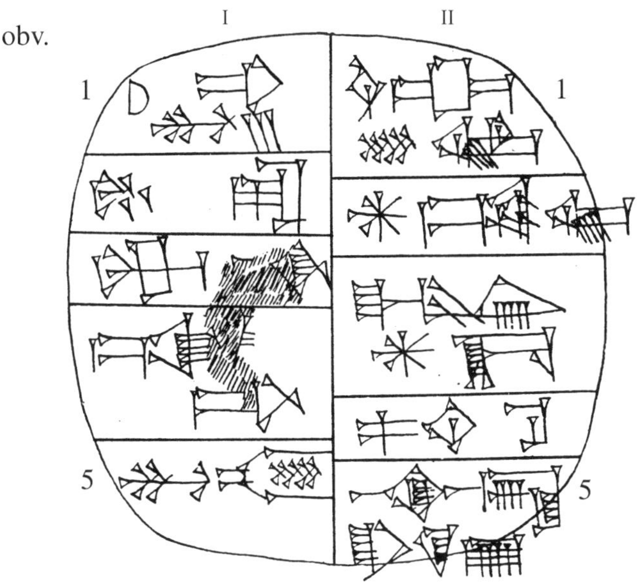

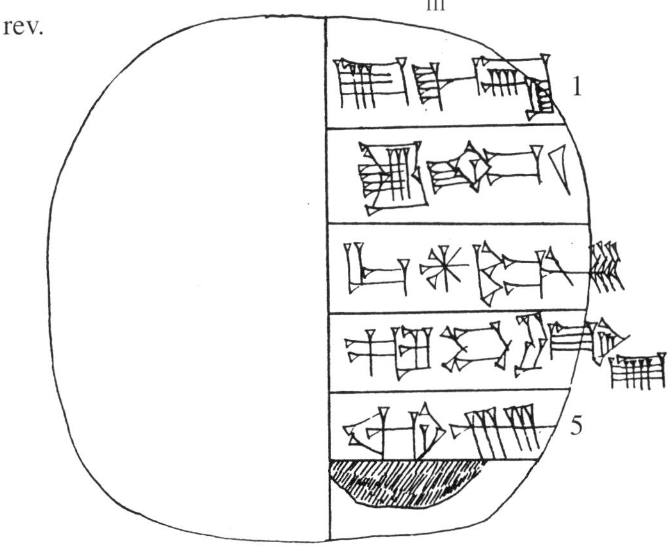

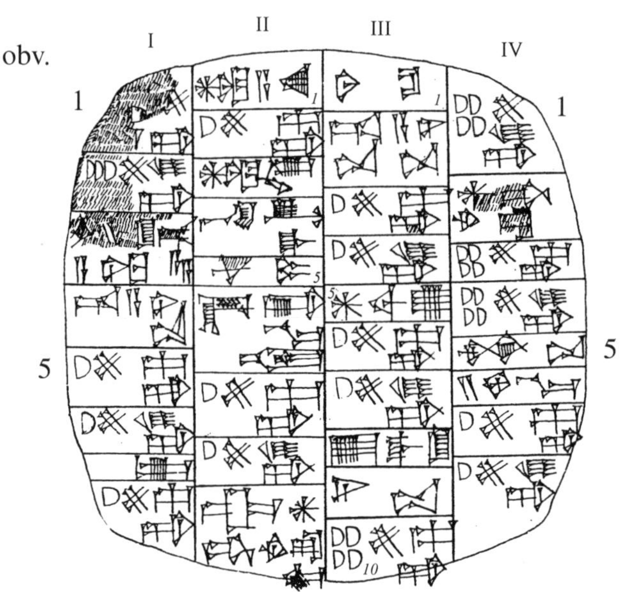
obv.
I
II
III
IV
1
5
1
5

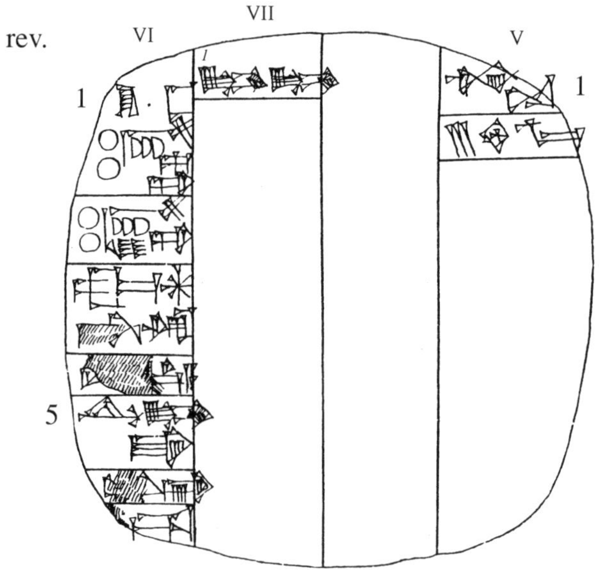
rev.
VI
VII
V
1
5
1

2. Sign List

This list is limited to the signs that occur in the texts in this book and arranges them, in the column on the right, according to their Neo-Assyrian order. It is to these numbers that the numbers in the alphabetically arranged List of Phonetic Values refer.

The second column to the right lists the values that the signs have in the texts in this book. The central column presents the signs in chronological order. It does not include every variant, since the same sign can be written somewhat differently within the same text. The forms are typical and intended to help the reader in identifying the signs.

Columns **M** and **B** refer to C. Mittermayer unter Mitarbeit von P. Attinger, Altbabylonische Zeichenliste der sumerisch-literarischen Texte (Fribourg/Göttingen 2006 [= OBO; Sonderband]) and R. Borger, Mesopotamisches Zeichenlexikon (Münster 2004; ^{2}2010 [= AOAT 305]). In the appendix, reference (**R**) is given to Y. Rosengarten, Répertoire commenté des signes présargoniques sumériens de Lagaš (Paris 1967).

M	B				
1	1		aš rum		1
303	14	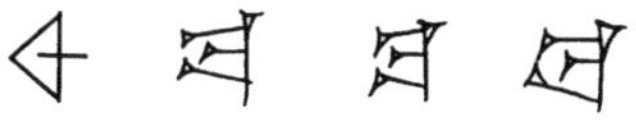	ba	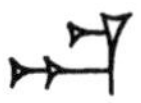	2
304	15		sú zu		3
304	15		abzu	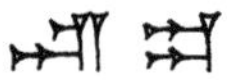	3a
305	16		kuš su		4
306	17	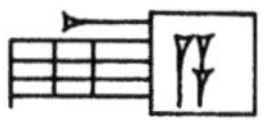	šen		5
3	5	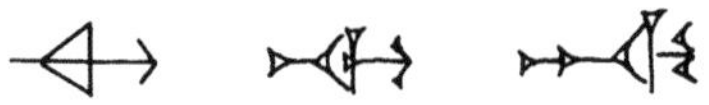	bala	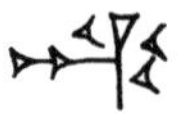	6
8	6	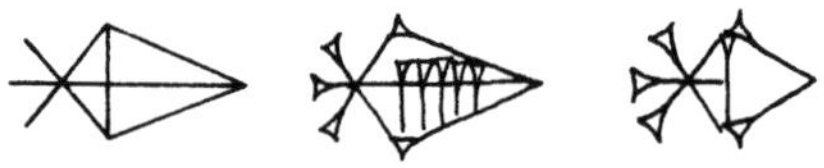	g̃ír g̃íri		7
13	8	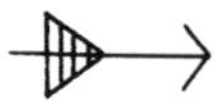	ušum		8
231	9	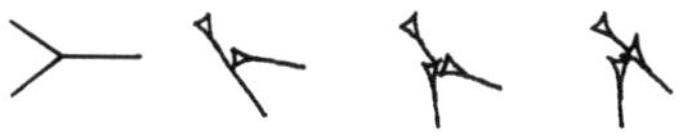	ku_5 sila tar		9
9	10		am_6 an dig̃ir		10

M	B			
312	24	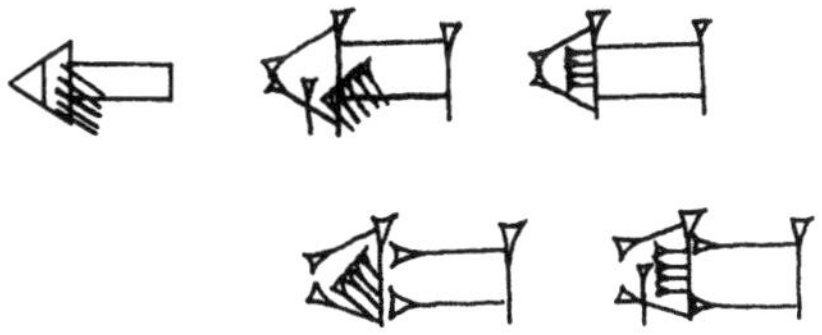	du$_{11}$ giri$_{17}$ gù inim ka zú	 11
312	24		[d]ištaran	 11a
329	65	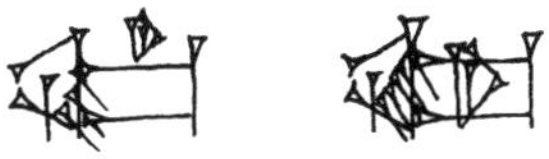	gu$_{7}$	 12
181	71		iri rí uru	 13
186	73	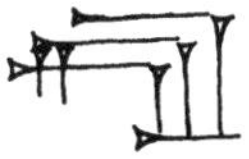	unken	 14
—	74	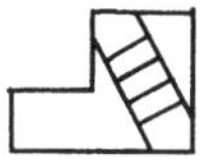	uru$_{11}$	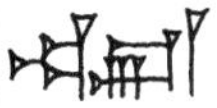 15
189	80		g̃ešgal u$_{18}$	 16
190	81	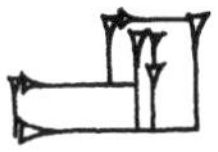	uru$_{18}$	 17
—	18		èr	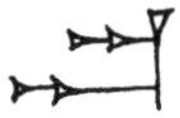 18

M	B			
17	19		úrdu	19
334	20		iti	20
4	22		subur	21
177	89		la	22
5	90		engar	23
6	91		maḫ	24
382	86		dú tu	
375	87		ku$_4$	
283	88		gur$_8$	25
381	85		èn le li	26
249	92		kúr	27

M	B			
249	96		pa$_5$	27a
20	98		g̃u$_{10}$ mu	28
269	99		sìla	29
269	99		sagi	29a
58	106		taka$_4$	30
250	105		gi$_{16}$	31
60	111		ru šub	32
25	113		til	33
24	110		na	34
28	115		nu$_{11}$	35
28	115		lagas[ki]	35a

M	B			
26	117		nuĝun	36
23	118		ti	37
57	121		bar	
29	120		maš	
—	120		1/2	38
19	112		nu	39
31	130		máš	40
34	132		ḫu mušen	41
42	134		nam	42
61	136		ĝál ig	43

M	B			
36	138		še$_{21}$	44
41	140		zi	45
150	103		ZI ZI .ŠÈ	ZI ZI .ŠÈ 45a
40	141		ge gi si$_{22}$	46
39	142		re ri	47
47	143		nun	48
47	143		eridu[ki]	48a
299	157		gada	49
300	159		akkil	50

M	B			
301	160		umbin	 51
15	168	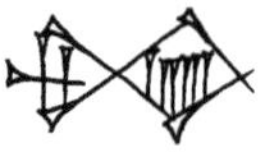	mun	 52
52	127	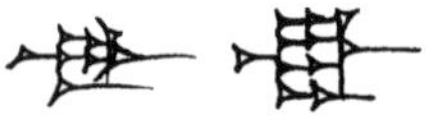	a_5 ak	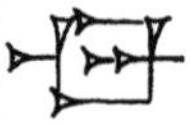 53
62	164	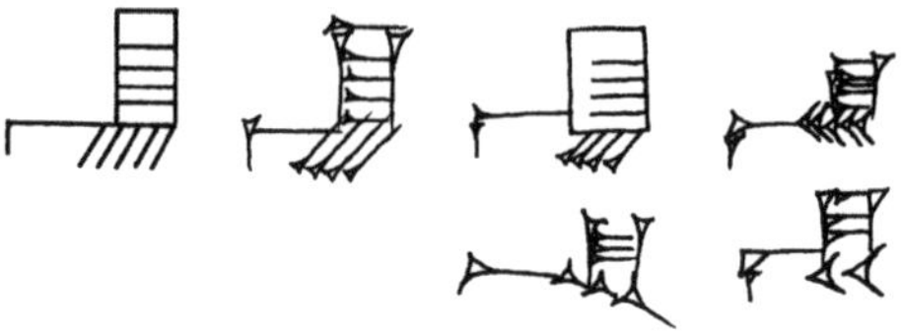	en uru_{16}	 54
62	164		^{d}sìn[1] ^{d}sîn ^{d}zuen	 54a
365	166	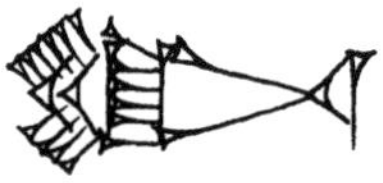	taraḫ	 55
56	151		sur	 56
44	153	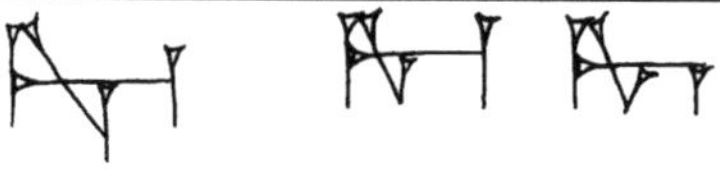	mùš	 57
44	153		^{d}inana	 57a
44	156		sùbi	 57b
147	172		sa	 58
443	173		ašgab	 58a

1 According to R. Borger, MesZL, p. 517 “lies lieber sîn” instead of sìn.

M	B			
106	174		aša$_5$ gána	
246	175		kára	59
89	176		gú	60
88	178		dur	61
—	178		duran	61a
92	180		gur	62
164	181		si	63
37	183		dar tár	64
309	184		sag̃	65
50	201		má	66
54	203		ud$_5$	67
164	207		diri	68

M	B			
110	215		límmu	69
121	221		tà	70
125	223		ab èš	71
10	247		mul	72
175	222		ká kan_4	73
113	238		um	74
112b	242		dub	75
123	248		ta	76
192	252		i	77
120	253		gan ḫé	78

M	B			
393	255	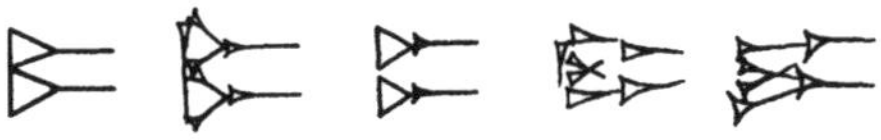	bànda dumu	 79
393	255		ibila	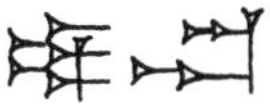 79a
132	258	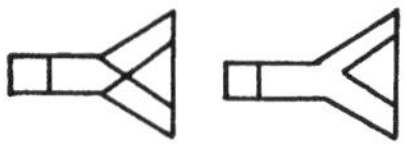	ad	 80
386	261	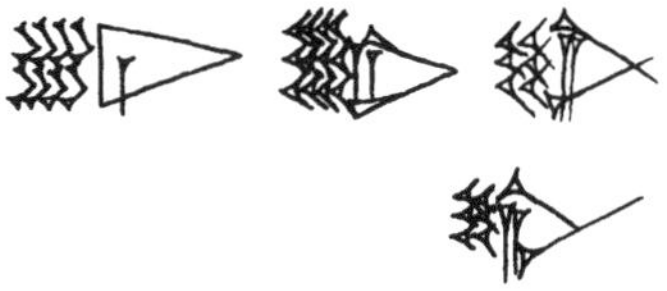	in	 81
221a	266	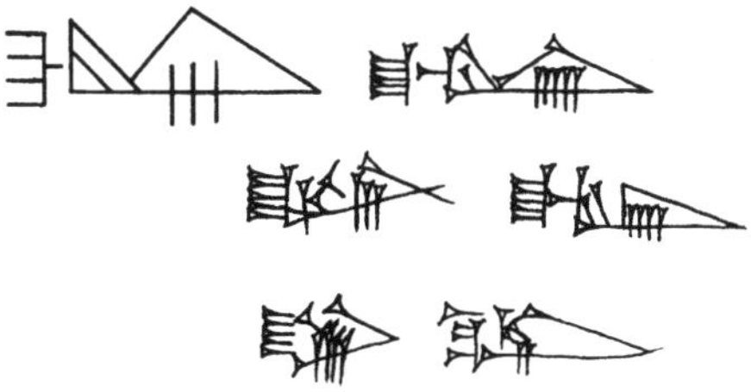	lugal	 82
152a	271		izim	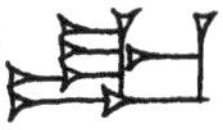 83
159	285		àsila	 84
153	275		bàd	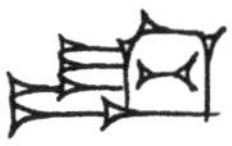
153	275	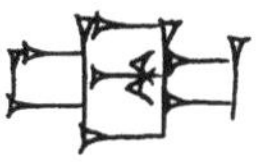	ug_5	85

M	B			
152c	271b		kéše	86
388	292		sì šúm	87
—	302		káš	88
141	298		du_8	89
115	300		eden	90
119	309		am	91
116	313		bí dè izi lim_4 ne	92
116	313		érim	92a
117	312		gibil	93
136	326		ág̃	94

M	B			
137	333		sa_{10} sám	 95
138	339	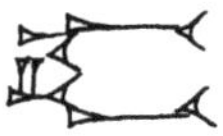	gum	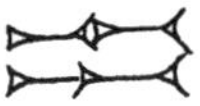 96
129	232		$guna_4$	 97
129	232		$unug^{ki}$	 97a
131	236		našše	 98
131	236		$ni\tilde{g}en_6{}^{ki}$	 98a
65	351	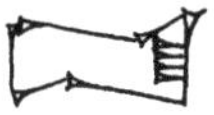	suḫuš	 99
66	352	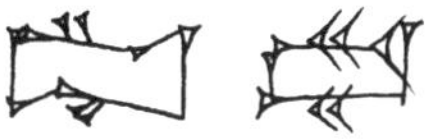	$kaš_4$ gir_5	 100
64	350	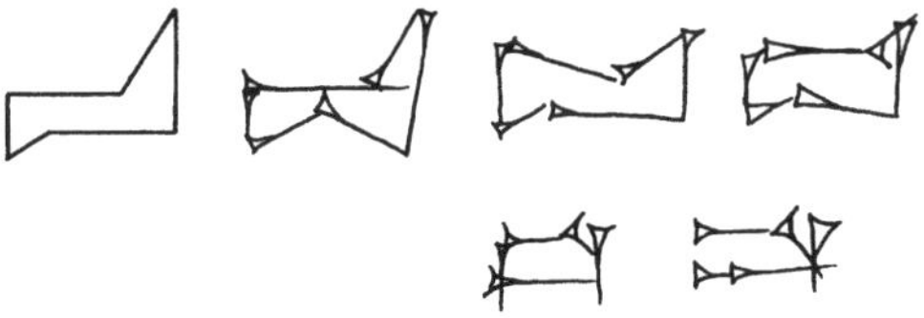	de_6 du gub g̃en rá re_6 túm	 101
64	350		$laḫ_5$	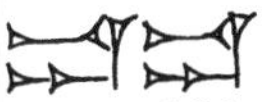 101a

M	B			
75	354		íb	102
292	353		anše	103
292	353		dùr	103a
77	212		g̃eštin	104
68	381		ninta ús uš	105
—	381		gala	105a
162	357		iš $kuš_7$ saḫar	106
79	358		bé bi pí	107
—	361		BI×NÍG̃	BI×NÍG̃ 107a
83	362		šem	108

M	B			
—	378		kib	109
262	385		na$_4$	110
260	379		dù gag rú	111
261	380		ì lé lí né ni zal	112
—	380		delmun[ki]	112a
263	437		ir	113
93	387		g̃á g̃e$_{26}$	114
270	388		šita	114a
94	392		ama dag̃al	115
96	397		g̃anun	116
161	435		kisal par$_4$	117

M	B			
97	408		sila$_4$	118
99	411		ùr uru$_{12}$	119
105	431		g̃alga	120
168	438		dag	121
143	464		g̃idru pa ugula	122
143	464		rig$_7$	122a
143	464		maškim	122b
143	466		sab	122c
143	464		énsi	122d
143	468		sipa	122e
160	469		g̃eš	123
385	541		$^{g̃eš}$kiri$_6$	123a
160	469		$^{g̃eš\text{-}tu_9}$g̃eštu	123b
160	469		$^{g̃eš}$g̃eštu^{tu_9}	123c

M	B			
118	472		gu$_4$	124
108	474		al	125
288	504		ub	126
144	483		mar	127
167	498		e	128
80	499		dug	129
86	499		báḫar	129a
169	501		kalam ùğ un	130
163	484		ke$_4$ líl	131
212	485		sağğa	132

M	B			
146	490		ú	133
201	491		ga gur_{11}	134
202	492		gára	134a
204	493		gùru íl	135
196	494		luḫ $sugal_7$	136
176	496		g̃uruš kala sig_{15}	137
176	496		^{na_4}esi	137a
107	495		é	138
107	495		asag̃	138a

M	B			
148	502		nir	139
214	507		ge_4	140
194	511		ra	141
253	514		lú	142
21a	535		urin	
21b	535		ses	143
21b	535		úri[ki]	143a
21b	535		uri_5[ki]	143b
22	535		[d]nanna	143c
206	540		zà	144
385	541		mú sar	145

M	B			
209	543		gàr gàra	146
230	560		á	147
229	561		da	148
215	547		dé	149
211	548		áš	150
166	552		ma	151
213	553		gal	152
213	553		ušumgal	152a
217	554		para$_{10}$	153
222	558		peš	154

M	B			
219b	556		niĝir	155
223	559		bur	156
203	566		ša	157
225	567		šu	158
225	567		tukum	158a
227a	568		kad_4	159
227b	569		kàm	159a
296	570		ka_5 lu_5 nar	160
228	571		sa_6	161
199	573		alan	162

M	B			
224	574		uri	 163
369	578		gìn kur	 164
378	579		še	 165
265	580	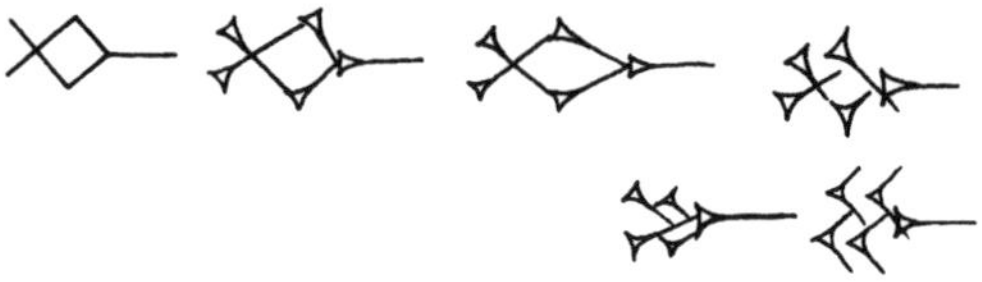	bu gíd pu sír su_{13}	 166
266	584		sù	 167
267	585		muš	 168
380	587	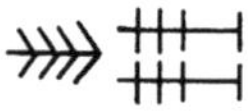	ter	 169
289	589		te temen	 170
289	589		unu_6	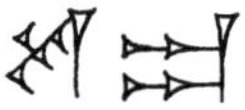 170a
290	590		kar	 170b

M	B			
332	596		babbar u_4 ud	171
332	596		ᵈutu	171a
332	596		bábbar dadag	171b
332	596		ararma[ki]	171c
332	596		è	171d
332	596		zimbir[ki]	171e
332	596		ⁱ⁷buranuna	171f
370	598		pi	172
433	599		šà	173
333	611		úḫ	174
247	612		érin	175
371	614		nunus	176
277	631 632		du_{10} šár	177
282	639		luḫša	178

M	B			
297	641		im ní	179
297	641		^{d}iškur	179a
9	641		ánzu^{mušen}	179b
281	644		ḫur	180
294	645		ḫuš	181
279	640		kam	182
337	661		bùr bùru šu$_4$ šuš u	
—	661		10	183
358	663		^{u}ugu$_6$	184
—	670		u-gùnu	185
—	670		^{d}eš$_{18}$-tár	185a

M	B			
352	672		áb	186
352	672		ùnu	186a
295	703		alim	187
348	681		gég gegge g̃e$_{6}$ mi	188
345	684		saman$_{4}$	189
364	689		g̃èšnu	190
355	690		nim	191
355	690		elam[ki]	191a
356	691		tùm	192
367	695		amar	193
—	695		[d]marduk	193a

M	B				
67	686	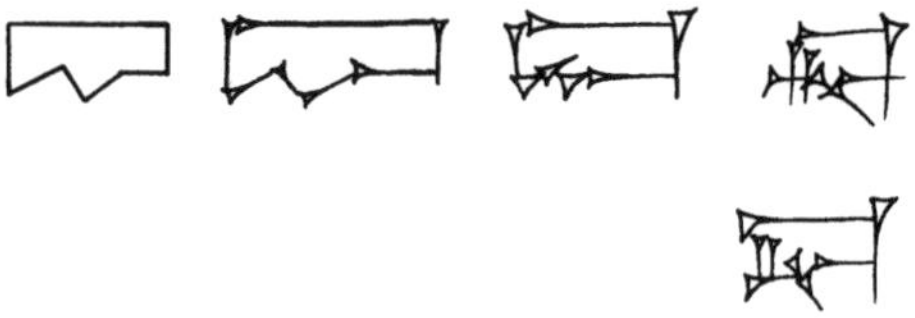	dím gen_7 šidim		 194
344	698	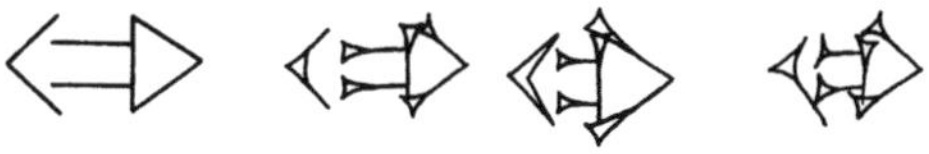	du_7 ul		 195
349	704	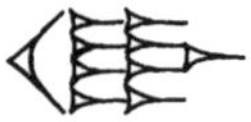	dugud		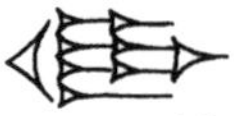 196
337	—		niĝar		197
—	—		niĝar[ĝar]		 197a
233	724		gi_8 igi ši		 198
235	725	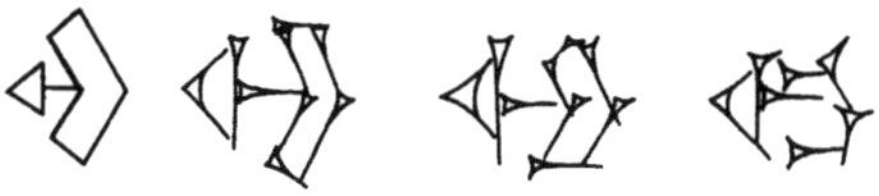	pà		 199
234	726		ar		 200
237	727	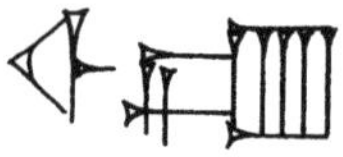	agrig		 201
239b	731		ù		 202
240	733		ḫulu		 203

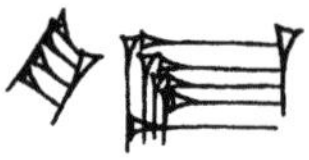

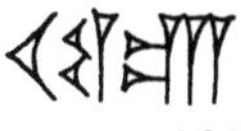

M	B			
431	736		di sá silim	204
360	720		dul	205
311	721		du_6	205a
311	721		e_{11}	205b
432	737		ki	206
438	744		sul	207
428	745		kù	208
366	711		eš ùšu 30	209
376	714		ninnu 50	210
390	748		deš 1 g̃éš 60	[2] 211
391	750		lá	212

2 This sign is also used to indicate the name of a person.

M	B			
402	755		ni$_{10}$ níĝen	213
404	756		engur namma	214
399	766		u$_{8}$	215
409	776		šára	216
410	786		gígir pú	217
414	795		abbar	218
403	804		kìlib	219
392	753		me	220
—	748		ĝéš-u 600	221
394	807		ib	222

M	B			
415	808		dúr dab$_5$ tuš	
417	809		dul$_5$ tu$_9$ umuš	[3]
420	810		éš šè úb	223
—	808		durun$_x$	223a
416	812		lu udu	224
447	815		kíĝ saga$_{11}$	225
395	816		siki	226
398	818		eren	227
422	869		šú	228
423	871		kèš	229

3 The readings of the signs KU / TÚG / ŠÈ given here are those that occur in the texts in this book. For further information about how to distinguish these signs in third millennium sources see R. Biggs, JCS 20 (1966) 77, fig. 1; 77f., note 37; 87, note 101; J. Krecher, WO 18 (1987) 18f.

M	B			
422	876		^{šú}šutul$_4$	230
450	883		munus	231
450	883		galla$_4^{\text{la}}$	231a
450	883		mussa	231b
452	887		nin	232
454	889		dam	233
459	890		géme	234
458	891		gu	235
449	893		nağar	236
457	896		kúšu	237
160	469		umma^{ki}	[4] 237a
455	899		sikil	238

4 This toponym is possibly to be read /ğiša^{ki}/, see *Place Names* s.v. umma^{ki}.

M	B			
248	900		lum núm	
243	906		g̃úrgu	239
243	905		šeg$_{12}$	240
465	825		min 2	241
439	826		šušana 1/3	242
—	838		kingusili 5/6	243
444	827		du$_{12}$ tuku	244
400	828		lik ur	245
470	839		a	246
470	839		àm	246a
470	839		i$_7$	246b
474	851		za	247
475	856		ḫa	248

M	B			
469	834		eš$_5$ 3	249
401b	836		àga giĝ$_4$	250
473	859		ĝar níĝ	251
476	861		ía 5	252
478	866		umun$_7$ 7	253

APPENDIX

CAPACITY MEASURES

	R 37		2 (bariga)	254

SURFACE MEASURES

	R 29		1 (bùr)	255
	31		60 "	256
	34		10 " (= bùr'u)	257

PRE-SARGONIC YEAR DATES (texts 33-34 and 40-44)

	—			258

3. List of Phonetic Values

This list contains the phonetic values in alphabetical order. The number accompanying each phonetic value refers to the number of its sign in our sign list. Given in parenthesis are the sign names.

a (A)	246
á (Á)	147
a$_5$ (AG)	53
ab (AB)	71
áb (ÁB)	186
abbar (SUG)	218
abzu (ZU.AB)	3a
ad (AD)	80
àga (GÍN)	250
agrig (AGRIG)	201
áĝ (ÁĜ)	94
ak (AG)	53
akkil (AKKIL)	50
al (AL)	125
alan (ALAM)	162
alim (ALIM)	187
am (AM)	91
àm (A.AN)	246a
am$_6$ (AN)	10
ama (AMA)	115
amar (AMAR)	193
an (AN)	10
anše (ANŠE)	103
ánzu (AN.IM.MI)	179b
ar (AR)	200
ararma (UD.UNUG)	171c
asaĝ (É.ŠE)	138a
àsila (ÀSILAL)	84
aš (AŠ)	1
áš (ÁŠ)	150
aša$_5$ (GÁN)	59
ašgab (AŠGAB)	58a

ba (BA)	2
babbar (UD)	171
bábbar (UD.UD)	171b
bàd (BÀD)	85
báḫar (BÁḪAR)	129a
bala (BAL)	6
bànda (TUR)	79
bar (BAR)	38
bé (BI)	107
bi (BI)	107
BI×NÍĜ (BI×NÍĜ)	107a
bí (NE)	92
bu (BU)	166
bur (BUR)	156
bùr (U)	183
buranuna (UD.KIB.NUN)	171f
bùru (U)	183

da (DA)	148
dab$_5$ (KU)	223
dadag (UD.UD)	171b
dag (DAG)	121
daĝal (AMA)	115
dam (DAM)	233
dar (DAR)	64
dé (DÉ)	149
dè (NE)	92
de$_6$ (DU)	101
delmun (NI.TUK)	112a
deš (DIŠ)	211
di (DI)	204
diĝir (AN)	10
dím (GIM)	194
diri (DIR)	68
du (DU)	101
dú (TU)	25
dù (GAG)	111
du$_6$ (DU$_6$)	205a
du$_7$ (UL)	195

du$_{8}$ (GAB) 89
du$_{10}$ (ḪI) 177
du$_{11}$ (KA) 11
du$_{12}$ (TUK) 244
dub (DUB) 75
dug (DUG) 129
dugud (DUGUD) 196
dul (DUL) 205
dul$_{5}$ (TÚG) 223
dumu (TUR) 79
dur (DUR) 61
dúr (KU) 223
dùr (ANŠE.ARAD) 103a
duran (DUR.KIB) 61a
durun$_{x}$ (KU.KU) 223a

e (E) 128
é (É) 138
è (UD.DU) 171d
e$_{11}$ (DU$_{6}$.DU) 205b
eden (EDIN) 90
elam (NIM) 191a
en (EN) 54
èn (LI) 26
engar (APIN) 23
engur (ENGUR) 214
énsi (PA.TE.SI) 122d
èr (ARAD) 18
eren (EREN) 227
eridu (NUN) 48a
érim (NE.RU) 92a
érin (ERIM) 175
esi (KAL) 137a
eš (EŠ) 209
éš (ŠÈ) 223
èš (AB) 71
eš$_{5}$ (EŠ$_{5}$) 249
eš$_{18}$-tár (GE$_{23}$.DAR) 185a

ga (GA) 134
gada (GAD) 49
gag (GAG) 111
gal (GAL) 152
gala (UŠ.KU) 105a
galla$_{4}$ (MUNUS) 231a
gan (GAN) 78
gána (GÁN) 59
gàr (GÀR) 146
gára (GÁR) 134a
gàra (GÀR) 146
ge (GI) 46
ge$_{4}$ (GI$_{4}$) 140
gég (MI) 188
gegge (MI) 188
géme (GÉME) 234
gen$_{7}$ (GIM) 194
gi (GI) 46
gi$_{8}$ (IGI) 198
gi$_{16}$ (GIL) 31
gibil (BÍL) 93
gíd (BU) 166
gígir (TÚL) 217
giğ$_{4}$ (GÍN) 250
gìn (KUR) 164
gir$_{5}$ (KAŠ$_{4}$) 100
giri$_{17}$ (KA) 11
gu (GU) 235
gú (GÚ) 60
gù (KA) 11
gu$_{4}$ (GU$_{4}$) 124
gu$_{7}$ (GU$_{7}$) 12
gub (DU) 101
gum (KUM) 96
guna$_{4}$ (UNUG) 97
gur (GUR) 62
gur$_{8}$ (GUR$_{8}$) 25
gur$_{11}$ (GA) 134
gùru (ÍL) 135

ğá (ĞÁ) 114
ğál (IG) 43
ğalga (ĞALGA) 120
ğanun (ĞANUN) 116
ğar (NÍĞ) 251
ğe$_{6}$ (MI) 188

g̃e$_{26}$ (G̃Á)	114
g̃en (DU)	101
g̃eš (G̃IŠ)	123
g̃éš (DIŠ)	211
g̃éš-u (DIŠ.U)	221
g̃ešgal (G̃IŠGAL)	16
g̃èšnu (NÁ)	190
g̃eštin (G̃EŠTIN)	104
g̃eštu (PI)	123b-c
g̃idru (PA)	122
g̃ír (G̃ÍR(-g.))	7
g̃íri (G̃ÍR(-g.))	7
g̃u$_{10}$ (MU)	28
g̃úrgu (MÚRGU)	239
g̃uruš (KAL)	137

ḫa (ḪA)	248
ḫé (GAN)	78
ḫu (ḪU)	41
ḫulu (ḪUL)	203
ḫur (ḪAR)	180
ḫuš (ḪUŠ)	181

i (I)	77
ì (NI)	112
i$_{7}$ (A.ENGUR)	246b
ía (ÍA)	252
ib (IB)	222
íb (TUM)	102
ibila (TUR.UŠ)	79a
ig (IG)	43
igi (IGI)	198
íl (ÍL)	135
im (IM)	179
in (IN)	81
inana (MÙŠ)	57a
inim (KA)	11
ir (IR)	113
iri (URU)	13
iš (IŠ)	106
iškur (IM)	179a
ištaran (KA.DI)	11a
iti (ITI)	20
izi (NE)	92
izim (EZEN)	83

ka (KA)	11
ká (KÁ)	73
ka$_{5}$ (LUL)	160
kad$_{4}$ (KAD$_{4}$)	159
kala (KAL)	137
kalam (UN)	130
kam (KAM)	182
kàm (KAD$_{5}$)	159a
kan$_{4}$ (KÁ)	73
kar (KAR)	170b
kára (KÁR)	59
káš (KASKAL)	88
kaš$_{4}$ (KAŠ$_{4}$)	100
ke$_{4}$ (KID)	131
kèš (KÈŠ)	229
kéše (KEŠDA)	86
ki (KI)	206
kib (KIB)	109
kíg̃ (KIN)	225
kìlib (NIG̃IN)	219
kingusili (KINGUSILA)	243
kiri$_{6}$ (SAR)	123a
kisal (KISAL)	117
kù (KUG)	208
ku$_{4}$ (KU$_{4}$)	25
ku$_{5}$ (TAR)	9
kur (KUR)	164
kúr (PAP)	27
kuš (SU)	4
kuš$_{7}$ (IŠ)	106
kúšu (KÚŠU)	237

la (LA)	22
lá (LAL)	212
lagas (NU$_{11}$.BUR.LA)	35a
laḫ$_{5}$ (DU.DU)	101a
le (LI)	26
lé (NI)	112

Value (Sign)	No.
li (LI)	26
lí (NI)	112
lik (UR)	245
líl (KID)	131
lim$_{4}$ (NE)	92
límmu (LÍMMU)	69
lu (LU)	224
lú (LÚ)	142
lu$_{5}$ (LUL)	160
lugal (LUGAL)	82
luḫ (LUḪ)	136
luḫša (GUDU$_{4}$.U)	178
lum (LUM)	239
ma (MA)	151
má (MÁ)	66
maḫ (MAḪ)	24
mar (MAR)	127
marduk (AMAR.UTU)	193a
maš (MAŠ)	38
máš (MÁŠ)	40
maškim (MAŠKIM)	122b
me (ME)	220
mi (MI)	188
min (MIN)	241
mu (MU)	28
mú (SAR)	145
mul (MUL)	72
mun (MUN)	52
munus (MUNUS)	231
mussa (MUNUS.UŠ.DI)	231b
muš (MUŠ)	168
mùš (MÙŠ)	57
mušen (ḪU)	41
na (NA)	34
na$_{4}$ (NA$_{4}$)	110
nağar (NAĞAR)	236
nam (NAM)	42
namma (ENGUR)	214
nanna (ŠEŠ.KI)	143c
nar (LUL)	160
naššе (NINA)	98
ne (NE)	92
né (NI)	112
ni (NI)	112
ní (IM)	179
ni$_{10}$ (LAGAB)	213
níğ (NÍĞ)	251
niğar (U.UD.KID)	197, 197a
níğen (LAGAB)	213
niğen$_{6}$ (NINA)	98a
niğir (MIR)	155
nim (NIM)	191
nin (NIN)	232
ninnu (NINNU)	210
ninta (UŠ)	105
nir (NIR)	139
nu (NU)	39
nu$_{11}$ (ŠIR)	35
nuğun (NUMUN)	36
núm (LUM)	239
nun (NUN)	48
nunus (NUNUZ)	176
pa (PA)	122
pà (PÀD)	199
pa$_{5}$ (PAP.E)	27a
par$_{4}$ (KISAL)	117
para$_{10}$ (BÁRA)	153
peš (GIR)	154
pi (PI)	172
pí (BI)	107
pu (BU)	166
pú (TÚL)	217
ra (RA)	141
rá (DU)	101
re (RI)	47
re$_{6}$ (DU)	101
ri (RI)	47
rí (URU)	13
rig$_{7}$ (PA.ḪÚB.DU)	122a
ru (RU)	32

rú (GAG) 111
rum (AŠ) 1

sa (SA) 58
sá (DI) 204
sa$_{6}$ (SA$_{6}$) 161
sa$_{10}$ (ŠÁM) 95
sab (ŠAB) 122c
saga$_{11}$ (KIN) 225
sagi (SÌLA.ŠU.GAB) 29a
sağ (SAĞ) 65
sağğa (ŠID) 132
saḫar (IŠ) 106
sám (ŠÁM) 95
saman$_{4}$ (ŠAGAN) 189
sar (SAR) 145
ses (ŠEŠ) 143
si (SI) 63
sì (SUM) 87
si$_{22}$ (GI) 46
sig$_{15}$ (KAL) 137
siki (SÍK) 226
sikil (EL) 238
sila (TAR) 9
sìla (SÌLA) 29
sila$_{4}$ (SILA$_{4}$) 118
silim (DI) 204
sîn (ZU.EN) 54a
sìn (ZU.EN) 54a
sipa (SIPA) 122e
sír (BU) 166
su (SU) 4
sú (ZU) 3
sù (SUD) 167
su$_{13}$ (BU) 166
sùbi (MÙŠ.ZA) 57b
subur (ŠUBUR) 21
sugal$_{7}$ (LUḪ) 136
suḫuš (SUḪUŠ) 99
sul (ŠUL) 207
sur (SUR) 56

ša (ŠA) 157
šà (ŠÀ) 173
šár (ḪI) 177
šára (ŠÁRA) 216
še (ŠE) 165
šè (ŠÈ) 223
še$_{21}$ (SA$_{4}$) 44
šeg$_{12}$ (SIG$_{4}$) 240
šem (ŠIM) 108
šen (ŠEN) 5
ši (IGI) 198
šidim (GIM) 194
šita (ŠITA) 114a
šu (ŠU) 158
šú (ŠÚ) 228
šu$_{4}$ (U) 183
šub (RU) 32
šúm (SUM) 87
šuš (U) 183
šušana (ŠUŠANA) 242
šutul$_{4}$ (DUN$_{4}$) 230

ta (TA) 76
tà (TAG) 70
taka$_{4}$ (KÍD) 30
tar (TAR) 9
tár (DAR) 64
taraḫ (DÀR) 55
te (TE) 170
temen (TE) 170
ter (TIR) 169
ti (TI) 37
til (BAD) 33
tu (TU) 25
tu$_{9}$ (TÚG) 223
tuku (TUK) 244
tukum (ŠU.NÍĞ.TUR.LAL) 158a
túm (DU) 101
tùm (TÙM) 192
tuš (KU) 223

u (U)	183
u-gùnu (U.DAR)	185
ú (Ú)	133
ù (Ù)	202
u$_4$ (UD)	171
u$_8$ (U$_8$)	215
u$_{18}$ (ĞIŠGAL)	16
ub (UB)	126
úb (ŠÈ)	223
ud (UD)	171
ud$_5$ (ÙZ)	67
udu (LU)	224
ug$_5$ (BÀD)	85
^{u}ugu$_6$ (U.KA [UGU])	184
ugula (PA)	122
ùğ (UN)	130
úḫ (ÚḪ)	174
ul (UL)	195
um (UM)	74
umbin (UMBIN)	51
umma (ĞIŠ.KÚŠU)	237a
umun$_7$ (IMIN)	253
umuš (TÚG)	223
un (UN)	130
unken (UKKIN)	14
ùnu (ÁB.KU)	186a
unu$_6$ (TE.AB)	170a
unug (UNUG)	97a
ur (UR)	245
ùr (ÙR)	119
úrdu (ÁRAD)	19
uri (URI)	163
úri (ŠEŠ.UNUG)	143a
uri$_5$ (ŠEŠ.AB)	143b
urin (ÙRI)	143
uru (URU)	13
uru$_{11}$ (URU×KÁR)	15
uru$_{12}$ (ÙR)	119
uru$_{16}$ (EN)	54
uru$_{18}$ (URU×A)	17
ús (UŠ)	105
uš (UŠ)	105
ùšu (EŠ)	209
ušum (BÚR)	8
ušumgal (GAL.BÚR)	152a
utu (UD)	171a

za (ZA)	247
zà (ZAG)	144
zal (NI)	112
zi (ZI)	45
ZI/ZI.ŠÈ (ZI/ZI.ŠÈ)	45a
zimbir (UD.KIB.NUN)	171e
zu (ZU)	3
zú (KA)	11
zuen (EN.ZU)	54a

Numerals

1/3	242
1/2	38
5/6	243
1	211
2	241
3	249
5	252
7	253
10	183
30	209
50	210
60	211
600	221

Capacity and Surface Measures

bariga	254
bùr	255-257

4. Glossary

This glossary is divided into the following parts:

The *General Vocabulary* consists of the words that appear in the texts contained in this book. It does not claim to give a detailed definition of each word, but rather the general sense. Particular meanings are given only when they are necessary to understand a particular passage; in such a case the passage in question is indicated, grammatical elements are not included among the words.

The Akkadian equivalents, when known, are placed next to each Sumerian word: naturally, the Akkadian words themselves do not appear in the Sumerian texts. Sumerian equivalents are placed next to each Akkadian word in the Akkadian glossary.

The use of hyphens within the *Glossary* as well as in the transliterations of the texts is conventional. For an outline of the underlying linguistic problem – the correct identification of word boundaries – see A.H. Jagersma, *A Descriptive Grammar of Sumerian* (https://openaccess.leidenuniv.nl/handle/1887/16107), 69-71, 4.2. "The Sumerological concept of 'Kettenbildung'".

Within the *General Vocabulary* the following grammatical terms and abbreviations are used:

ḫamṭu/marû (*ḫ./m.*): for a discussion of these Akkadian grammatical terms used to describe aspects of the Sumerian verb, see P. Attinger, *Éléments de linguistique sumérienne. La construction de du$_{11}$/e/di «dire»* (Fribourg/Göttingen 1993 [= OBO; Sonderband]) § 119 and § 120; D.O. Edzard, *Sumerian Grammar* (Leiden/Boston 2003 [= HdO I 71]) 73f., 12.2.

R = word root

cf. (confer) is a way of indicating that the Akkadian represents an equivalent, although such an equation does not explicitly appear in the ancient texts. It also indicates a semantic relationship rather than a translation.

4.1 General Vocabulary

4.1.1 Sumerian

a (*mû*)	water
(amar-)a-a-si-ge$_4$-da	see amar-R-R-si-ge$_4$-da
a-ga (cf. *warkatum*)	back room
-a-ni (*-šu*/*-ši*)	his; her (3. sg. person); (-a)-ni is read (-a)-né in southern Old Sumerian; see V. Meyer-Laurin, ZA 100 (2010) 9, note 27
a-ra-zu (*teslītum*)	prayer
(x) a-rá (*adi* [x] / [x]-*ī-šu*)	x times (x is a numerical value)
a--ru (*šarākum*)	to dedicate
á (*idum*)	arm; strength; power; rent (31:2)
á--áĝ (*wârum* D)	to give a command or an instruction
á-...-ta	at the prompting of; by means of the strength of
a$_5$	see AK
áb (*littum*)	cow
abbar (*appārum*)	swamp; cane-brake
abzu (*apsûm*)	see *Sacred Buildings*
ad-da (*abum*)	father
áĝ (*madādum*)	to measure (by means of capacity)
(á--)áĝ	see á--R
(ki--)áĝ	see ki--R
àga-kára--sì(-g)	to strike with a weapon; to conquer (see J. Klein, Studies Tadmor, 310f.)
àga-ús (*rēdûm*)	policeman
agrig (*abarakkum*)	steward; an important temple administrator
AK (*epēšum*)	to do; for the different orthographical forms and readings (/a$_5$/; /a-k/; /ak/; /k/; /kè/) of the relevant conjugated and nonconjugated *ḫamṭu* and *marû*-forms of AK see P. Attinger, ZA 95 (2005) 47-64
(níĝ--)AK-(AK)	see níĝ--R-(R)
(šu-gibil--)AK	see šu-gibil--R
akkil (*ikkillum*)	lamentation
al (*allum*)	hoe
alan (*ṣalmum*)	statue
alim (*ditānum*, *kusarikkum*)	bison
ama (*ummum*)	mother
ama-ar-gi$_8$ (*andurārum*)	freedom? (gi$_8$ is a graphic variant of ge$_4$); lit.: "to return to mother"; see C. Wilcke, EANEL, 1.1.1; 1.1.3; 1.1.6
amar (*būrum*)	young calf; foal; kid
amar-a-a-si-ge$_4$-da	see *Festivals*

an (*šamû*)	heaven; sky
an-ub-da (*kibrātum*)	regions; "quarters"
anše (*imērum*)	donkey
asag̃ (É.ŠE) (*qarītum*)	storeroom; for É.ŠE = a/esag̃ see J. Krecher, Studies Matouš II, 36; Å. Sjöberg, ZA 83 (1993) 15f.
àsila (*rīštum*)	joy
aša$_5$(-g) (*eqlum*)	a plot of land; see GÁNA
ašgab (*aškāpum*)	leather-worker
ba (*qiāšum*)	to donate
(šu--)ba	see šu--R
ba-al (*ḫerûm*)	to dig a canal; to channel
babbar/bábbar (*namrum*; *peṣûm*)	shining; white
(kù-)babbar/bábbar	see kù-R
bàd (*dūrum*)	wall
(šeg$_{12}$-)BÁḪAR	see šeg$_{12}$-R
bala (*palûm*)	term of office; reign; dynasty
(nu-)bànda	see nu-R
bar (igi-g̃ál-ni)	see note on igi-g̃ál
(igi--)bar	see igi--R
(igi zi--)bar	see igi zi--R
bariga ('UL'; *pars/šiktum*)	a measure of capacity (ca. 60 l.; see M. Powell, RlA 7, 492-496; 497 § IV.5)
-bi (*-šu/-ši*)	its (3. sg. non-person); -bi is read -bé in southern Old Sumerian; see V. Meyer-Laurin, ZA 100 (2010) 9, note 27
-bi-da(-ke$_4$) (*u*)	and
(tukum-)bi	see tukum-R
[lú]BI×NÍG̃ (*sirāšûm*)	brewer (see P. Steinkeller, FAOS 17, 291)
(é-)BI×NÍG̃	see *Sacred Buildings*
bùr (*būrum*)	a surface measure (Akkadian loanword): 1 bùr = 3 eše = 18 iku = 1800 s/šar (see M. Powell, RlA 7, 480f. § II.11)
bùru(-d) (*palāšum*)	to pierce
da(-g)	nearness (to someone; see J. Krecher, ASJ 9 [1987] 88, note 39)
dab$_5$ (*ṣabātum*)	to seize; to take; to take away
(di--)dab$_5$	see di--R
dadag (*namrum*)	bright; shining; pure
(g̃á-la--)dag	see g̃á-la--R

dağal 1. (*rapšum*)	wide
2. (*rapāšum* D)	to broaden
(šu-)dağal--(du$_{11}$)	see šu-R--du$_{11}$
dam (*aššatum*)	wife
(kù) dam-(taka$_{4}$)	see kù R-taka$_{4}$
dam-gàra (*tamkārum*)	merchant (Akkadian loanword)
(^{d}nin-)dar	see *Divine Names*
(gù--)dé	see gù--R
de$_{6}$ 1. (*wabālum* [*ḫ*.: de$_{6}$; *m*.: túm])	to bring; to deliver
2. (*tabālum* [*ḫ*.: túm; *m*.: tùm])	to carry off; to lead away (for the varying *ḫamṭu*/*marû* paradigms of this lexem in the third millennium see V. Meyer-Laurin, ZA 100 [2010] 1-14)
deš (*ištēn*)	one
di ([*marû* participle of du$_{11}$(-g)] *qabûm*)	to say; to speak
di--dab$_{5}$ (*dīnam šūḫuzum*)	to take up a lawsuit; for a discussion of this term see E. Dombradi, FAOS 20/1, § 224 and §§ 421-423
di-ku$_{5}$ 1. (*dajjānum*)	judge
2. (*dīnum*)	judgment
di--ku$_{5}$(-d^{r}) (*dīnam diānum*)	to pass judgment
di til-la (*dīnum gamrum*)	law case for which a final decision has been given
diğir 1. (*ilum*)	god; divinity
2.	determinative for divine beings
dím (*epēšum*)	to build; to make
(kù-)dím	see kù-R
diri-...-šè	beyond
du	see ğen
DU	see de$_{6}$; du; gub; ğen; túm
(šu-du$_{8}$-a--)DU	see šu-du$_{8}$-a--R
DU.DU	see laḫ$_{5}$
du-rí (*dārûm*)	everlasting; enduring
(mun-)du	see mun-R
dú(-d) (*walādum*)	to give birth; to create (a statue 21 III 9-10; 22 III 2-3); the reading given follows PEa 684-685 tu-ú [= *marû*?] and du-ú [= *ḫamṭu*?]; see J. Krecher, AOAT 240, 160f.
dù [*d^{r}u] (*banûm; epēšum*)	to build; to construct; to erect (see W. Heimpel, CUSAS 5, 235-237)
(ğíri--)dù	see ğíri--R
(ğeš--)dù	see ğeš--R
du$_{7}$ (*wasmum*)	fitting; suitable; necessary

(ḫé-)du$_7$	see ḫé-R
(šu--)du$_7$	see šu--R
du$_8$ 1. (*labānum*)	to spread; to mould bricks
2. (*peḫûm*)	to coat with pitch; to caulk
(šu-)du$_8$-(a--DU)	see šu-R-a--DU
(igi-nu-)du$_8$	see igi-nu-R
du$_{10}$(-g) (*ṭābum*)	good; favourable; pleasing
du$_{11}$(-g) (*qabûm; dabābum* [*ḫamṭu*])	to say; to declare; see e
(sá--)du$_{11}$-du$_{11}$	see sá--R-R
(šu-dag̃al--)du$_{11}$	see šu-dag̃al--R
(šu-tà(-g)--)du$_{11}$	see šu-tà--R
du$_{11}$-ga (*qibītum*)	pronouncement; statement; speech (29:7)
dub (*ṭ/tuppum*)	tablet; document
(sag̃-)dub	see sag̃-R
dub-šen (*tupšinnum*)	a type of chest that serves as a treasure-box (see J. Bauer, AoN 1985, 20-22, n. 29; M. Civil, AulOr 5 [1987] 20f.)
dug (*karpatum*)	jug; vessel
(èš-)dug-(ru)	see *Sacred Buildings*
dugud (*kabtum*)	heavy; important
dul (*katāmum*)	to cover
dul$_5$ (*katāmum*)	to cover (dul$_5$ is the graph used in pre-Sargonic texts such as in 18 II 4. It is later replaced by dul)
dumu 1. (*mārum*)	child; son
2. (*mārtum*)	daughter
dumu-dú-da	son of (lit.: "son born (of)")
dumu-KA	grandson (see Å. Sjöberg, HSAO, 209-212)
dumu-munus (*mārtum*)	daughter
[g̃eš]dúr-g̃ar (*kussûm; durga(r)rû*)	chair; throne (see H. Waetzoldt, RlA 8, 327f., § 5.2)
dùr (*mūrum*)	foal
dùr-KAŠ$_4$ (*šānûm*)	donkey foal (the reading of KAŠ$_4$ is uncertain, see MSL VIII/1, 52: 380-381)
durun	to place (objects [15 III 3]); for KU.KU = durun$_x$ (plural form of the *ḫamṭu*-base tuš) see P. Attinger, N.A.B.U. 2010/65
(ú-)durun$_x$	see ú-R
e (*qabûm* [*marû*])	to say; see du$_{11}$(-g)
é (*bītum*)	house; temple (see the names in *Sacred Buildings*); plot of land
é-gal (*ekallum*)	palace

é-munus	women's residence (see K. Maekawa, Mesopotamia 8/9 [1973-1974] 77-144)
è ([*ḫamṭu*; *marû*: è(-d)] *waṣûm* G, Š)	to (let sth./smb.) go out; to come out; to lead out; to bring out; to appear (as a witness)
(pa--)è	see pa--R
e_{11}(-d) (*warādum* Š)	to bring down; to fetch; in 21 r.sh. I 1 e_{11}(-d) combined with the prefix /-ta-/ means "to cede"
eden (*edinu; ṣērum*)	steppe; plain
(gú-)eden-(na)	see gú-R-na
en 1. (*enum*)	a kind of priest; a partner in the sacred marriage rite
2. (*bēlum*)	lord
(ki-)en-(gi(-r))	see ki-R-gi(-r)
en-nu (*maṣṣartum*)	guard; watchpost (for the reading en-nu(-ùĝ) see J. Krecher, Studies Matouš II, 37; see also [en]-⌜nu⌝ = [*ma*]-*ṣa-ar-tum* [MSL XIII, 38 iv 15])
(saĝ-)èn-(tar)	see saĝ-R-tar
engar (*ikkarum*)	farmer
engar gu_4-ra	ox-driving farmer; farmer (and) oxherd (see H. Steible, FAOS 9/2, 54f.)
énsi (*iššiakkum*)	city ruler; viceroy (see G. Marchesi/N. Marchetti, MC 14, 109-113)
énsi-gal	chief steward (see G. Marchesi/N. Marchetti, MC 14, 109)
$^{(ĝeš)}$eren (*erēnum*)	cedar(wood)
eren bábbar (*ti(')āl/rum*)	white cedar(wood)
(nam-)érim	see nam-R
(nam-)érim--(ku_5(-d^r))	see nam-R--ku_5(-d^r)
(nam-)érin	see nam-R
^{na_4}esi (*ušûm*)	diorite (as in [all? of] Gudea's statues); olivine-gabbro (see W. Heimpel, RA 76 [1982] 65-67; ZA 77 [1987] 48f.; K. Leslie, ZA 92 [2002] 296-300)
eš (= $eš_5$; *šalāš*)	three (36:4)
èš (*bītum*)	sanctuary (see CAD B, 282, lexical section)
$eš_5$ (*šalāš*)	three

ga (*šizbum*)	milk (see M. Stol, RlA 8, 189-201)
(na-)gada	see na-R
^{ĝeš}gag-si-sá (*šiltāḫum*)	arrow
gal 1. (*rabûm*)	big; mighty; great
2.	chief (34 VI 4)
gal-zu (*mūdûm*)	wise; intelligent

(é-)gal	see é-R
(énsi-)gal	see énsi-R
gala (*kalûm*)	liturgical singer (see J. Krecher, SKLy, 27f., 35f.); the archaic spelling of gala was G̃ÈŠ.DÚR "penis + anus" (see P. Steinkeller/J.N. Postgate, MC 4, 37)
$galla_4$[la] (*ūrum*)	female sexual organs; vulva
gan (*wālittum*)	"which have born or can bear" (said of females)
(má-)gan[ki]	see *Place Names*
GÁNA (*eqlum*)	a plot of land; for GÁNA(-g) = $aša_5$(-g) see M. Civil, JCS 25 (1973) 171ff. and M. Powell, ibid., 178ff.
ge_4 (*târum* G, D)	to return; to bring back; to take up a case again
(ki-bé--)ge_4-(ge_4)	see ki-bé--R-R
(šu--)ge_4	see šu--R
gég (*ṣalmum*)	dark
(káš) gég	see káš R
-gen_7 (*kīma*)	like (comparative)
gi (*apum; qanûm*)	reed
gi-gù-na (*gigunûm*)	a sacred building ("reed chamber"; see *Sacred Buildings*)
gi-$guna_4$	a sacred building ("reed chamber"); see gi-gù-na
gi(-n // gi-in) (*kânum* G, D)	to be firm; to make firm; to be steadfast; to be stable; to fix; to award; with ka-g.a: to agree with a statement
(ki-en-)gi(-r)	see ki-en-R
(ama-ar-)gi_8	see ama-ar-R
gi_{16}-sa (*dārûm, dārītum*)	lasting; of lasting value
(šu-)gibil--(AK)	see šu-R--AK
gíd (*šadādum*)	to drag; to tow; to measure; to manage (38:7)
(má-)gíd	see má-R
$gig̃_4$ (*šiqlum*)	shekel (a unit of weight, ca. 8.333 g.; see M. Powell, RlA 7, 510 § V.4)
[g̃eš]gígir (*narkabtum*)	wagon; chariot
$giri_{17}$ (*appum*)	nose; the conventional reading /kìri/ is most likely only appropriate for texts from northern Babylonia (Kiš, Sippar(?); see MSL XIV, 110, 1.1 i' 4'; VS 10 101 rev. 1), whereas PEa Nippur indicates a reading /giri/ (= $giri_{17}$); see PEa 305; 418
$giri_{17}$ šu--g̃ál (*appam labānum*)	to greet and entreat (lit.: "to let the hand be at the nose"; see U. Magen, BaF 9 [1986] 60-61; 104-108)
[g̃eš]gu-za (*kussûm*)	throne; chair (see H. Waetzoldt, RlA 8, 327f.)
gu-za-lá (*guzalûm*)	chair-bearer; throne-bearer

gú-eden-na	see *Place Names*
gú g̃eš--g̃ál	to provide a delivery of wood
gù--dé (*nabûm*)	to call; to name
gu_4(-d^r) (*alpum*)	steer; ox
(engar) gu_4-(ra)	see engar R-ra
gu_7 (*akālum*)	to eat; to suck (milk); to enjoy the usufruct of something
(níg̃-)gu_7-(a)	see níg̃-R-a
gub ([*ḫamṭu*/*marû*] *izuzzum* G, Š)	to stand; to set up
(gi-)gù-n(a)	see gi-R
(gi-)$guna_4$	see gi-R
gur (*târum* G, D)	to return; to give back
(má-)gur_8	see má-R
(níg̃-)gur_{11}	see níg̃-R
g̃á-la--dag (*naparkûm*)	to stop working (see P. Steinkeller, FAOS 17, 66-68)
^{d}g̃á-tùm-du_{10}(-g)	see *Divine Names*
g̃á $^{g̃eš}$ù-šub-ba (*nalbanum*)	brick making shed (see D.A. Foxvog, N.A.B.U. 1998/7); brick mould (see W. Heimpel, CUSAS 5, 195)
g̃ál--$taka_4$ (*petûm*)	to open
(igi-(x-))g̃ál	see igi-(x-)R
(nir-)g̃ál	see nir-R
(zi-)g̃ál-(la)	see zi-R-la
($giri_{17}$ šu--)g̃ál	see $giri_{17}$ šu--R
(gú g̃eš--)g̃ál	see gú g̃eš--R
(zi-šà-)g̃ál	see zi-šà-R
g̃alga (*milkum*)	advice
g̃anun (*ganūnum*)	storehouse; granary
g̃ar (*šakānum*)	to set; to put
($^{g̃eš}$dúr-)g̃ar	see $^{g̃eš}$dúr-R
(igi--)g̃ar	see igi--R
(NE.NE-)g̃ar	see NE.NE-R
(sá-)g̃ar	see sá-R
$g̃e_6$-par_4 (*gipa(r)ru*)	see *Sacred Buildings*
g̃en ([*ḫ*., singular/*m*.: du] *alākum*)	to go
g̃eš 1. (*iṣum*)	tree; wood
2.	determinative for wooden objects
g̃eš-dù-a	timber (see H. Steible, FAOS 9/2, 43f.)
g̃eš--ḫur (*eṣērum*)	to make a drawing; to design
g̃eš-ḫur (*uṣurtum*; *gišḫu(r)ru*)	cultic rule or ordinance (see G. Farber-Flügge, St. Pohl 10, 181f.; ead., AulOr 9 [1991] 85f.)

ĝeš-kíĝ-ti (*kiška/ittû*)	craftsman
ĝeš--tà(-g) (cf. *gištaggû*)	to offer
(gú) ĝeš--(ĝál)	see gú R--ĝál
(ì-)ĝeš	see ì-R
ĝéš (*šūši*)	sixty
ĝéš-u (*nēru*)	six hundred
^{ĝeš}ĝèšnu (*eršum*)	bed; see H. Waetzoldt, RlA 8, 326f.
ĝeštin (*karānum*)	grape juice; bunch of grapes
$^{\text{ĝeš-tu}_9}$ĝeštu(-g)/ ^{ĝeš}ĝeštu$^{\text{tu}_9}$(-g) 1. (*uznum*)	ear
2. (*ḫasīsum*)	understanding; wisdom
ĝidru (*ḫaṭṭum*)	sceptre
(^{d}nin-)ĝír-(su/sú)	see *Divine Names*
ĝíri--DÙ	to cut off(?); to carve out(?)
-ĝu$_{10}$ (*-ī/-ja*)	my (1. sg.)
ĝúrgu-...-ta	after
ĝuruš (*eṭlum*)	an adult; young man; recruit; worker
(ne-)**ḫ**a	see ne-R
ḫa-la (*zittum*)	lot; assigned portion
ḫa-lu-úb (*ḫa/uluppum*)	oak(?) (see J.N. Postgate, BSA 3, 135; 146; M. Van De Mieroop, BSA 6, 159; 182)
ḫé-du$_7$ (*wusmum*)	decoration
ḫé-ĝál (*ḫe(n)gallum; ṭuḫdum*)	overflow; abundance
ḫulu (*šulputum*)	to destroy; to ruin; for a discussion of the verb /ḫul/ ↔ /ḫulu/ see J. Krecher, AOAT 240, 192f., with note 103
(ĝeš-)ḫur	see ĝeš-R
(ĝeš--)ḫur	see ĝeš--R
ḫur-saĝ (*ḫuršānum*)	hill country; mountainous region
ḫuš (*ḫuššûm; ruššûm*)	red; terrifying
i (= è)	to come out; to appear (in the phrase u$_4$ ul-lí-a-ta); there seems to be a semantic relation between /i/ and /è/, but it is uncertain whether /i/ and /è/ can be considered identical verbs
ì (*šamnum*)	vegetable oil; animal fat
ì-bí-la (*aplum*)	heir (syllabic writing of ibila)
ì-du$_8$ (*atûm*)	porter; door keeper
ì-ĝeš (*ellum; šamnum*)	sesame oil
i$_7$(-d) 1. (*nārum*)	river; canal
2.	determinative for rivers and canals

ía (*ḫamiš*)	five
ibila (*aplum*)	heir (Akkadian loanword?)
ig (*daltum*)	(panel of a) door
igi (*īnum*)	eye; glance
igi-...-šè (*maḫar*)	in the presence of (said about witnesses at a trial)
igi--bar (*amārum; naplusum*)	to look at (see J. Krecher, Kutscher Memorial Vol., 108-111)
igi-(x-)g̃ál	a phrase used to express fractions (see J. Friberg, RlA 7, 535f. § 3.1); the phrase bar igi-g̃ál-ni (38:5) is difficult to define
igi--g̃ar	to appear before someone (37:3); for this use of igi--g̃ar, corresponding to the Akkadian *pānī šakānum*, see E. Dombradi, FAOS 20/1, § 402
igi-nu-du$_8$(-a)	helper; unskilled worker (see G.J. Selz, FAOS 15/1, 72 1:1; W. Heimpel, KASKAL 6 [2006], 43-48)
igi zi--bar (*kīniš naplusum*)	to choose; to legitimate (lit.: "to look at sb. favourably")
íl (*našûm*)	to lift; to bring; to convey; to endure
(sag̃--)íl	see sag̃--R
im (*ṭīdum*)	clay; loam
inim (*awātum*)	word; statement; decree (the reading /inim/ is conventional; other sources suggest a reading /enem/, /enim/ or /inem/; see J. Bauer, WO 39 [2009] 250)
inim-ma--sì(-g)	to keep to the word (lit.: "to place in a word"; see M. Civil, Studies Birot, 75)
(lú) inim-(ma)	see lú R-ma
(lú ki-)inim-(ma)	see lú ki-R-ma
ir (*erī/ēšum*)	fragrance; scent; fragrant
iri 1. (*ālum*)	city; district (in early sources rather read /eri/)
2.	determinative of cities
iti (*warḫum*)	month (for the individual month names see the index in M.E. Cohen, Cultic Calendars, 483-499)
izi (*išātum*)	fire
izi--lá	to purify with fire (see J. Bauer, AfO 40/41 [1993/94] 95; for a reading bí--lá, "to spread smoke", see J. Krecher, OrNS 54 [1985] 147, note 31)
izim (*isinnum*)	festival; feast; for particulars about the festivals that appear in texts 41-44, see the information in *Festivals*

ka-al(-ak) (cf. *kalakkum*)	loam pit (23 ii 22; 25 ii 14; see D.A. Foxvog, N.A.B.U. 1998/7)
ka(-g) (*pûm*)	statement (in the expression ka.g- ... -a--gi(-n) [37:11; 38:29]; see J. Krecher, ZA 69 [1979] 1-3)
ka-saman$_4$	chief oil-maker (see P. Steinkeller, FAOS 17, 200)
(dumu-)KA	see dumu-R
ká (*bābum*)	gate (the reading /ká/ is conventional; according to other sources it should rather be /kan$_4$/ or /ákan/)
kala(-g) (*dannum*)	strong; mighty
kalam (*mātum*)	land (specifically, Sumer)
kàm (*nakārum* D)	to overturn; to change (29:7)
kar (*kārum*)	quay
(àga-)kára--(sì(-g))	see àga-R--sì(-g)
káš (*šika/ārum*)	beer (fermented barley); alcoholic beverage (see CAD Š/II, 428, discussion section)
káš gég	dark beer
káš sig$_{15}$	light beer (see M. Powell, HANE/S 6, 104-106)
(dùr-)KAŠ$_4$	see dùr-R
kéše(-d^r) (*keš(e)d^r/*kšed^r) (*rakāsum*)	to bind (see A. Cavigneaux/F. Al-Rawi, ZA 85 [1995] 36, note 8)
(zú--)kéše(-d^r)	see zú--R
ki 1. (*ašrum*)	place; location; area; world
2.	determinative for place names
ki-...-ta	disbursed by (lit.: "from the place of")
ki--áĝ 1. (*râmum*)	to love; to show affection
2. (*narāmum*)	beloved
ki-bé--ge$_4$-(ge$_4$) (*ana ašrīšu turrum*)	to restore (lit.: "to return to its place")
ki-en-gi(-r; *kenĝir)	the land of Sumer (what the Sumerians called their land); see *Place Names*
(lú) ki-(inim-ma)	see lú R-inim-ma
ki-tuš (*šubtum*)	dwelling
ki-uri	the land of Akkade (uri <*war*(*i*); what the Sumerians called Akkade); see *Place Names*
(ĝeš-)kíĝ-(ti)	see ĝeš-R-ti
kìlib (*napḫarum*)	totality
kingusili (*parasrab*)	five-sixths
(nu-)kiri$_6$(-k)	see nu-R
kisal (*kisallum*)	courtyard
kiše$_4$ (*muttatum*)	half (in 39:21 it refers to the hair on the head)
kù(-g) 1. (*elēlum* D)	to purify; to make cultically pure
2. (*ellum*)	shining; bright; pure
3. (*kaspum*)	silver (for the semantic range of /kù-(g)/ see D.O. Edzard, CM 7, 160, note 5)
kù-babbar/bábbar (*kaspum*)	silver

kù dam-taka$_4$ (*uzubbûm*)	divorce settlement
kù-dím (*kuttimmum*)	silversmith
kù luḫ (*kaspum mesûm*)	refined silver
kù-si$_{22}$ (*ḫurāṣum*)	gold (see Å. Sjöberg, JCS 40 [1988] 174)
(ù--)ku$_4$	see ù--R (this verbal root must be distinguished from ku$_4$(-r) because it can appear as ù--ku)
ku$_4$(-r <d^r) (*erēbum* G, Š)	to (let sth./smb.) enter; to bring in (see J. Krecher, ZA 77 [1987] 7-10; 17-21 [palaeography of KU$_4$])
ku$_5$(-d^r) (*nakāsum*)	to cut
(di-)ku$_5$(-d^r)	see di-R
(nam--)ku$_5$(-d^r)	see nam-R
(nam-érim--)ku$_5$(-d^r)	see nam-érim--R
(še-saga$_{11}$-)ku$_5$(-d^r)	see še-saga$_{11}$-R
(umbin--)ku$_5$(-d^r)	see umbin--R
kur 1. (*šadûm*)	mountain; mountain range
2. (*mātum*)	land
kúr (*nakārum*)	to change
kuš (*maškum*)	skin (41 I 5)
kuš$_7$ (*kizûm*)	groom (see A. Cavigneaux, N.A.B.U. 1992/103; a reading /sùš/ instead of /kuš$_7$/ seems also possible)
lá 1. (*šaqālum*)	to weigh; to pay; to bear (in gu-za-lá)
2. (*maṭi*)	minus
(izi--)lá	see izi--R
laḫ$_5$ (DU.DU; *m.* plural; see de$_6$)	to lead towards (used for a plural object)
(má-)lah$_5$	see má-R
(me-)lim$_4$	see me-R
límmu (*erbe*)	four
lu (*balālum*)	to mix
lú (*awīlum*)	person; man
lú inim-ma (*šībum*)	witness (see C. Wilcke, EANEL, 8.1.1.5)
lú ki-inim-ma (*šībum*)	witness (see C. Wilcke, EANEL, 8.1.1.5; 8.1.3.1.2)
lú má-gur$_8$	boat captain
lú níĝ-tuku (cf. *rāšûm*)	creditor (lit.: "a person who has something")
(nam-)lú-(inim-ma)	see nam-R-inim-ma
lugal 1. (*šarrum*)	king
2. (*bēlum*)	master; owner
(mu) lugal	see mu R
(mu) lugal--(pà(-d))	see mu R--pà(-d)
(nam-)lugal	see nam-R
(kù) luḫ	see kù R
(šu)-luḫ	see šu-R
(^{d}šul-)luḫša	see *Divine Names*

ma-na (*manûm*)	mina (a unit of weight, ca. 500 g.; see M. Powell, RlA 7, 510 § V.5)
má (*eleppum*)	ship
má-gíd	(the one) who tows the barge (full of first-fruits to Enlil at Nippur; epithet of Gudea in 24 I 9)
má-gur$_8$ (*makurrum*)	cargo boat
(lú) má-(gur$_8$)	see lú R-gur$_8$
má-laḫ$_5$ (*malāḫum*)	sailor
maḫ (*ṣīrum*)	exalted; high
(sugal$_7$-)maḫ	see sugal$_7$-R
maš (*ṣibtum*)	produce; interest
maš/máš (*lalûm; urīṣum*)	kid; he-goat
maškim (*rābiṣum*)	commissioner (see D.O. Edzard/F.A.M. Wiggermann, RlA 7, 449-452)
me 1. (*bašûm*)	to be
2. (*mû; parṣum*)	divine power that makes the institutions of heaven and earth function (see G. Farber-Flügge, RlA 7, 610-613)
me-lim$_4$ (*melemmum*)	terrifying glance (lit.: "shining [divine] power")
min (*šina*)	two
mu 1. (*šumum*)	name
2. (*šattum*)	year
mu-...-a(k)-šè	because (in a nominalized sentence)
mu lugal	see mu lugal--pà(d)
mu lugal--pà(-d)	to swear by the king (lit.: "to call the king's name", corresponding to the Akkadian *nīš šarrim zakārum* "to pronounce the king's life"; mu lugal in 37:4 is an abbreviation for mu lugal--pà)
mu--pà(-d) ([*šumam*] *zakārum*)	to choose (lit.: "to name [someone]"; said about a ruler chosen by a divinity)
mu-sar-ra (*mus/šarû*)	(royal) inscription
mu-šè--še$_{21}$	to name; to give as name
mu-ús-sa (*šanītum šattum*)	the following year
mu-x	year-x (indicates a date according to a notable event that took place during the year)
mú (*waṣûm* Š)	to make sth./smb. grow
mul (*nabāṭum* G, Š)	to (let sth./smb.) shine
mun-du	morning offering (see J. Bauer, AWL, 411 ad I 1; CAD M/II, 202f., disc. section; L. Milano, RlA 8, 25 sub 3)
munus (*sinništum*)	woman (possibly to be read /munuš/)
(dumu-)munus	see dumu-R
(é-)munus	see é-R
(níĝ-)mussa	see níĝ-R

mušen 1. (*iṣṣūrum*)	bird
2.	determinative for birds
na ([in na-rú-a] *abnum*)	stone (22 III 2; 23 III 16, IV 17; 26 II 7); na is the original graph for the word 'stone' (usually written na_4); see P. Steinkeller, BiOr 52 (1995) 707; according to R. de Maaijer/B. Jagersma, AfO 50 (2003/2004), 354f. /na/ in alan-na simply refers to the final /n/ of /alan/
na-gada (*nāqidum*)	herdsman (Akkadian loanword)
na-rú-a (*narûm*)	stele (lit.: "set up, erected stone")
(ma-)na	see ma-R
na_4 1. (*abnum*)	stone
2.	determinative for minerals and stones
nag̃ar (*nagārum*)	carpenter
nam-	element used to form abstracts, such as English -hood, -ship, and -scape
nam-érim (*māmītum*)	assertory oath
nam-érim--ku_5(-d^r)	to take an assertory oath
nam-érin	assertory oath (variant writing of nam-érim; see A. Falkenstein, NG 1, 64, note 2)
nam--ku_5(-d^r) (*nazārum*)	to curse
nam-lú-inim-ma (*šībūtum*)	the act of witnessing
nam-lugal (*šarrūtum*)	kingship
nam-nin (*bēlūtum*)	rulership; position of supreme power
nam-nir-g̃ál (*muttallūtu*)	distinction; superiority
nam-šita	prayer (29:24; see H. Behrens/H. Steible, FAOS 6, 250f.)
nam-tar (*šīmtum*)	destiny
nam--tar (*šiāmum*)	to decree a destiny
nam-ti(-l) (*balāṭum*)	life
nar (*nārum*)	musician
ne-ḫa (*nēḫtum*)	rest (Akkadian loanword)
NE.NE-g̃ar	the fifth month in the Ur III calendar. Its Babylonian equivalent was the month *abum* (see G.J. Selz, N.A.B.U. 1989/38; M. Cohen, Cultic Calendars, 100-104)
(-a)-ni	see -a-R
ní (*puluḫtum*)	awe (based on unorthographic writing rather read /ne/)
ní--tuku 1. (*palāḫum*)	to experience awe or fear
2. (*na'dum*)	awesome (see M.-J. Seux, Épithètes royales, 430f.)

ní--te(-g̃) (*palāḫum*)	to fear; to respect
níg̃ (*ša*)	a thing; something; a matter
níg̃-AK-AK (*epištum*)	deed; activity
níg̃-gu_7-a (*ukultum*)	consumption; food consumed
níg̃-gur_{11} (*makkūrum*)	possession; property
níg̃-mussa (*te/irḫatum*)	wedding gift (see C. Wilcke, Familiengründung, 252-267; id., EANEL, 61, note 186)
níg̃-sám (*šīmum*)	price (see C. Wilcke, EANEL, 77f., 8.1.1.1)
(lú) níg̃-(tuku)	see lú R-tuku
níg̃-ú-rum (*makkūrum*)	possession; acquisition
níg̃-ul (*ša ṣiātim*)	what is fit for the cult (lit.: "what is primordial"; for the reading /ul/ rather than /du_7/ see Å. Sjöberg, OrSc 22 [1973] 116; J.S. Cooper, AnOr 52, 139; 166)
níg̃en 1. (*lawûm*)	to surround
2. (*saḫārum*)	to turn around; to go around; the *marû*-form NÍG̃IN.NÍG̃IN (39:24) is most likely to be read ni_{10}-ni_{10} (/*ne/inni/, see J. Krecher, Studies Matouš II, 53; 71, note 80; id., AOAT 240, 162; P. Attinger, ZA 88 [1998] 165, note 5)
(šu-)níg̃en	see šu-R
nig̃ir (*nagīrum*)	herald
nin (*bēltum*)	lady; mistress
(nam-)nin	see nam-R
ninnu (*ḫam/nšā*)	fifty
(nam-)nir-g̃ál	see nam-R
ninta (*zikarum*)	male; manly
(sag̃-)ninta	see sag̃-R
(udu-)ninta	see udu-R
nu-bànda (*laputtûm*)	inspector; overseer; captain (see P. Attinger, ÉLS, 156f., § 98 b) 1°)
nu-$kiri_6$(-k) (*nukarippum*)	gardener (for the etymology of the Akkadian *nukaribb/ppum* see M. Krebernik, BFE, 330)
(en-)nu	see en-R
(igi-)nu-(du_8)	see igi-R-du_8
nug̃un (*zērum*)	seed
nun 1. (*rubûm*)	prince
2. (*rabûm*)	great; princely
3.	fine (a quality of scent)

pa--è (*wapûm* Š)	to let sth./smb. shine
pà(-d) (*nabûm*)	to call; to name
(mu lugal--)pà(-d)	see mu-lugal--R

(mu--)pà(-d)	see mu--R
(šà(-ge)--)pà(-d)	see šà(-ge)--R
pa$_5$ (*palgum*)	ditch; canal
(ĝe$_6$-)par$_4$	see ĝe$_6$-R
pú (*būrtum*)	fountain
ra (*maḫāṣum*)	to beat; to drive (said of yoked animals; see H. Steible, FAOS 9/2, 54f.)
(engar gu$_4$-)ra	see engar R-ra
(du-)rí	see du-R
(šu-)rí	see šu-R
(saĝ--)rig$_7$	see saĝ--R
(a--)ru	see a--R
ru(-g)	to receive; to bring back (see G.J. Selz, ASJ 17 [1995] 274, note 103)
rú [*d^{r}u, see dù] (*banûm*)	to raise up; to set up
(na-)rú-(a)	see na-R-a
(ú-)rum	see ú-R
sa (*riksum*)	bundle
sá-du$_{11}$ (*šattukkum*)	regular offering
sá--du$_{11}$-du$_{11}$	to provide regular offerings
sá-ĝar (*mālikum*)	adviser; counsellor
(^{ĝeš}gag si-)sá	see ^{ĝeš}gag si-R
(si--)sá-sá	see si--R-R
sa$_6$(-g) 1. (*damqum*)	good
2. (*ṭābum*)	beautiful; fruitful
sa$_{10}$(-m) (*šâmum*)	to buy (see C. Wilcke, EANEL, 77, 8.1.1.1; 79, 8.1.1.6)
^{dug}sab (*šappum*)	pot; vessel
(še-)saga$_{11}$--(ku$_5$)	see še-R--ku$_5$
sagi (*šāqûm*)	cup-bearer (Akkadian loanword; see J.-J. Glassner, RlA 8, 420-422)
saĝ 1. (*rēšum*)	head; an architectural feature
2. (*rēštum*)	first-class
3. (*rēštûm*)	first; first-class
saĝ-dub	full worker (see W. Heimpel, CUSAS 5, 85); the meaning of saĝ-dub in 36:3 remains doubtful, see A. Falkenstein, NG 2, 213, note to 3
saĝ-èn-tar (*pāqidum*)	overseer; guardian
saĝ--íl (*rēšam ullûm*)	to raise; lit.: "to lift the 'head' (of a wall or temple)"; 28:13-14; 29:30

sağ-ninta (*rēšum*)	(grown) man (see P. Steinkeller, FAOS 17, 130f.)
sağ--rig$_{7}$ (*šarākum*)	to donate (sağ/sa$_{12}$--rig$_{7}$ may be a loan from the Akkadian *šarākum*)
sağ-šu$_{4}$ (*kubšum*)	cap (see H. Waetzoldt, RlA 6, 200f.)
sağ-ús (*rēšam kullum*)	to be available; to care for the maintenance of sth. or smb. (see M.-J. Seux, Épithètes royales, 440)
(ḫur-)sağ	see ḫur-R
(ur-)sağ	see ur-R
sağğa (*šangûm*)	temple-administrator
saḫar (*eperum*)	dirt; earth (see W. Heimpel, CUSAS 5, 189f.)
(níğ-)sám	see níğ-R
(ka-)saman$_{4}$	see ka-R
sar 1. (*šaṭārum*)	to write
2. (*mus/šarum*)	a surface measure: 1 s/šar = 60 gig̃$_{4}$ = 1/100 *ikûm* (see M. Powell, RlA 7, 479 § II.5)
(mu-)sar-(ra)	see mu-R-ra
ses (*aḫum*)	brother
si-(si(-g)) (*malûm* D)	to fill in
(àsila--)si-si	see àsila--R-R
si-sá (*išarum*)	right; legal
si--sá-sá (*ešērum* Š; Št)	to get ready (24 III 2); to yoke (25 III 12-13)
(^{ğeš}gag) si-(sá)	see ^{ğeš}gag R-sá
sì(-g/k) (*šakānum*)	to set (according to J. Krecher, AOAT 240, 195, the verbal roots sì(-g) and sì(-k) must be distinguished)
(àga-kára--)sì(-g)	see àga-kára--R
(kù-)si$_{22}$	see kù-R
(káš) sig$_{15}$	see káš R
siki (*šīpātum*)	wool
(udu-)siki	see udu-R
sikil (*ellum*)	pure; virginal
sìla (*qûm*)	a capacity measure; litre-vessel; in Pre-Sargonic Lagas as well as in the standard Akkad/Old Babylonian system 1 sìla equals approximately 1 litre (see M. Powell, RlA 7, 497 § IV.4-5)
sila$_{4}$ (*puḫādum*)	lamb
sipa(-d) (*rē'ûm*)	shepherd
(é-tar-)sír-(sír)	see *Sacred Buildings*
(pa$_{5}$-)sír-(ra)	see *Place Names*
su (*zumrum*; *šīrum*)	body; flesh (28:7, 24); as for 39:13 su/kuš = *zumrum/maškum* must be taken into consideration; see A. Cavigneaux/F. Al-Rawi, ZA 83 (1993) 202-205
(^{d}nin-ğír-)su/sú	see *Divine Names*

sù-sù(-g)	to satisfy? (34 v 1; this translation is based on the context; sù-sù(-g), literally "to make empty", remains difficult)
sù(-d^{r})/su$_{13}$(-d^{r}) (*arākum* G, D)	to be long; to lengthen
sùbi (cf. *namrum*)	shining (like the colour of the sùbi-stone [agate?]; for the variant readings /š/suba/, /subi/ see Å. Sjöberg, JCS 40 [1988] 172f., note 6)
sugal$_{7}$ (*šukkallum*)	courier; a high-ranking official
sugal$_{7}$-maḫ (*sukkalmaḫḫu*)	a high court official
suḫuš (*išdum*)	foundation (in early sources rather read /suḫus/; see J. Bauer, WO 39 [2009] 250)
(ù-)sur-ra	see ù-R
ša	element used in fractions
šà(-g) (*libbum*)	heart; content; interior
šà(-ge--)pà(-d)	to choose (lit.: "to call in the 'heart'")
šà-bi-ta	from it (lit.: "from its inside")
(zi-)šà-(g̃ál)	see zi-R-g̃ál
šár(-šár) (*dešûm* D)	to make abundant
še (*še'um*)	grain; barley
(mu-šè--)še$_{21}$	see mu-šè--R
še-ga (*migrum*)	favourite (see M.-J. Seux, Épithètes royales, 448-450)
še-saga$_{11}$-ku$_{5}$(-d^{r})	the twelfth month in the Ur III calendar; its Babylonian equivalent was the month *a(d)daru* (see M. Cohen, Cultic Calendars, 119-124; for the reading /saga$_{11}$/ instead of /gur$_{10}$/ see M. Civil, FI, 170f.)
šeg$_{12}$ (*libittum*)	sun-dried brick (see W. Heimpel, CUSAS 5, 191-193)
šeg$_{12}$-BÁḪAR(-ra) (cf. *agurrum*)	baked brick (possibly to be read šeg$_{12}$-alur$_{x}$-ra; see P. Steinkeller, JNES 52 [1993] 145; W. Heimpel, CUSAS 5, 193-195)
šem 1. (*rīqum*)	scent; fragrance
2.	fragrant
3.	determinative for perfumes
(dub-)šen	see dub-R
šidim (*itinnum*)	mason; builder (see W. Heimpel, CUSAS 5, 47f.)
(nam-)šita	see nam-R
šu (*qātum*)	hand; control
šu--ba(-d^{r}/r) (*wuššurum*)	to release (see J. Krecher, Kutscher Memorial Vol., 111-117)
šu--du$_{7}$-du$_{7}$ (*šuklulum*)	to complete; to finish
(giri$_{17}$) šu--(g̃ál)	see giri$_{17}$-R--g̃ál

šu--ge$_4$	to lead back; to bring back; to give back
šu--tà(-g) (*za'ānum* D)	to decorate; to adorn
šu--ti (*leqûm*)	to receive
šu--ùr (*pašāṭum*)	to erase (an inscription; lit.: "to flatten the hand [on something]")
šu-dağal--du$_{11}$	to supply abundantly with sth.
šu-du$_8$-a--DU(de$_6$/túm)	to act as guarantor for (see C. Wilcke, EANEL, 113, 113f., 8.5.2.1)
šu-gibil-gibil--AK	to renew
šu-luḫ (*šuluḫḫum*)	purification ritual (see G. Farber-Flügge, St.Pohl 10, 191-196; W.G. Lambert, RlA 4, 97f.)
šu-níğen (*napḫarum*)	total
šu-rí (*mišlānu*)	half (see J. Friberg, RlA 7, 536 § 3.1)
šu-tà(-g)--du$_{11}$ (*za'ānum* D)	to sprinkle (in 23 III 8-10 and 25 III 3-5 it is said about oil [ì] and fine scent [ir nun])
(sağ-)šu$_4$	see sağ-R
(ğá ^{ğeš}ù-)šub-(ba)	see ğá ^{ğeš}ù-R-ba
^{šú}šutul$_4$ (*nīrum*)	yoke
šúm (*nadānum*)	to give; to hand over; to lend
(zà--)šuš	see zà--R
šušana (*šuššān*)	one third

(ki-...-)**t**a	see ki-...-R
(ğúrgu-...-)ta	see ğúrgu-...-R
(ğeš--)tà(-g)	see ğeš--R
(šu--)tà(-g)	see šu--R
(šu-)tà(-g)--(du$_{11}$)	see šu-R--du$_{11}$
(ğál--)taka$_4$	see ğál--R
(kù dam)-taka$_4$	see kù dam-R
(nam--)tar	see nam--R
(sağ-èn-)tar	see sağ-èn-R
(é-)tar-(sír-sír)	see *Sacred Buildings*
taraḫ (*turāḫum*)	mountain goat
(má) taraḫ (abzu)	see má R abzu
(ní--)te(-ğ)	see ní--R
temen (*temmēnum*)	foundation peg (see S. Dunham, RA 80 [1986] 31-64)
ter (*qištum*)	forest; grove
(ğeš-kíğ-)ti	see ğeš-kíğ-R
(šu--)ti	see šu--R

ti(-l) (*balāṭum*)	to live (the form a-ba-ti-la:da "as long as he lives" in 38: 6 is difficult to explain. C. Wilcke, Care of the Elderly, 50, translates "while he was still alive")
(nam-)ti(-l)	see nam-R
til (*gamārum*)	to destroy; to exterminate
(di) til-(la)	see di R-la
tu	see dú(-d)
(^{d}nin-)tu(-r)	see *Divine Names*
tu_9 (*ṣubātum*)	garment; clothing
tuku (*ḫamṭu*; *marû*: du_{12}-du_{12})	
1. (*išûm*)	to have; with the infix /-da-/: to have a claim against somebody (30:5, 8)
2. (*aḫāzum*)	to marry
(lú níĝ-)tuku	see lú níĝ-R
(ní-)tuku	see ní-R
tukum-bi (*šumma*)	if; in case
túm	see de_6
(^{d}ĝá-)tùm-(du_{10}(-g))	see *Divine Names*
tuš ([*ḫamṭu*] *wašābum* G, Š)	to cause to dwell; to settle (for the plural form of this verb see durun)
(ki-)tuš	see ki-R
ú (*šammum*)	grass; a plant
ú-a (*zāninum*)	provider; supplier (see M.-J. Seux, Épithètes royales, 456-458)
ú-$durun_x$-na	brushwood(?); hay(?); for a discussion of this term (oven-grass?) see J. Bauer, OBO 160/1, 538
ú-rum	possession (see C. Wilcke, EANEL, 67, 6.1.1.3)
(^{d}ba-)Ú	see *Divine Names*
ù--ku_4 (*ṣalālum*)	to sleep; to rest (see (ù--)ku_4)
(ĝá) ^{ĝeš}ù-šub-ba	see ĝá R
ù-sur-ra (*ṣertum*)	sideburn(?); in 39:21 applied to pubic hair; for a discussion of this term as a variant of ù-/ú-sar see M. Civil, CUSAS 17, 263, note 77
u_4 (*ūmum*)	day
u_4-...(-a) (*inu*)	when
u_4-ba (*ina ūmīšu*)	at that time; then
u_4-bi-ta	the past (lit.: "from those days")
u_4 šú-uš-e (*ūmišam*)	daily; day by day; (from) day to day
u_4 ul-lí-a-ta (*ištu ūm ṣiātim*)	from long ago (for the meaning of ul and /i/ in this expression see J. van Dijk, AcOr 28 [1964] 33)
u_8 (*laḫrum*)	ewe

u_{18}-ru (*ṣīrum*; *elûm*)	exalted; high (see M.-C. Ludwig, SANTAG 2, 107-113)
ub (*tubqum*)	corner; a small room
(an) ub-(da)	see an R-da
ud_5 [*uzd] (*enzum*)	goat (see A. Cavigneaux, SAZ, 55f.; J. Bauer, AoN 1987, 2, n. 31; for the proposed reading /uzud/ see G. Selz, WO 26 [1995] 196)
udu (*immerum*)	sheep
udu-ninta (*immerum*)	ram
udu-siki	wool-producing sheep
ùg̃ (*nišū*)	people; population
(^{d}nin-te-)ug_5(-ga)	see *Divine Names*
$^{u}ugu_6$ (*eli*)	on; over
ugula (*waklum*)	chief; overseer (Akkadian loanword)
ul (cf. *ullûm*)	distant (in time, either past or future)
(níg̃-)ul	see níg̃-R
(u_4) ul-(lí-a-ta)	see u_4 R-lí-a-ta
umbin--ku_5(-d^{r}) (*gullubum*)	to shave; to shear (lit.: "to pluck with the fingernail")
$umun_7$ (*sebe*)	seven
umuš (*ṭēmum*)	decision; understanding (29 I 6)
unken (*puḫrum*)	assembly (<*ùg̃-kíg̃, lit.: "seeking [= consulting] the people")
ùnu(-d) (*utullum*)	cowherd (see G.J. Selz, FAOS 15/2, 86f.)
unu_6 (*mūšabum*; *šubtum*; *mākālum*)	living room; dining room? (where the gods received their food offerings); sanctuary (see A. Falkenstein, OrNS 35 [1966] 239-246; D. Charpin, clergé, 337f.)
ur (*kalbum*)	dog; for the meaning of ur in personal names like ur-^{d}DN see R. Di Vito, StPohl SM 16, 116f.; for Akkadian PN's containing the element *kalbum* see CAD K, 72 i)
ur-sag̃ (*qarrādum*)	hero
(šu--)ùr	see šu--R
úrdu(-d) (*wardum*)	slave; servant; subordinate
uri (*akkadûm*)	Akkadian
(ki-)uri	see ki-R
urin (*urinnum*)	standard
uru_{12}	the reading uru_{12} expresses the verbal root ùr (see šu--ùr) plus the verbal ending /-e/
uru_{16}(-n) (*dannum*; *naklum*)	strong; clever (see M. Civil, Studies Sjöberg, 55)
ús 1. (*redûm*)	to (make sth./smb.) follow
2. (*emēdum*)	to border on; when said about ships, to dock
(sag̃-)ús	see sag̃-R

uš (*uššum*)	foundation; pit(?)
(àga-)ús	see àga-R
(^{d}ama-)ušumgal-(an-na)	see *Divine Names*
za-gìn (*uqnûm*)	lapis-lazuli
(^{ĝeš}gu-)za	see ^{ĝeš}gu-R
zà(-g)--šuš (cf. *šimtum*)	to brand; to mark (see D. Foxvog, ZA 85 [1995] 1-3)
zal 1. (*šutebrûm*)	to pass
2. (*nasāḫum*)	when said about dating, u_4-x zal-la means "on the xth day"
zi(-d) (*kīnum*)	true; lawful, right; legitimate; legitimising; noble
zi-ĝál-la (*šiknat napištim*)	living being
zi šà-ĝál (*zišagallu*)	divine encouragement; inspiration (see J. Klein, ThŠH, 151 ad 52)
zi(-r) (*pasāsum* D)	to destroy; to annihilate
-zu (*-ka*/*-ki*)	your (2. sg.)
(gal-)zu	see gal-R
(a-ra-)zu	see a-ra-R
zú--kéše (cf. *kaṣārum*; *rakāsum*)	to obligate (smb. for sth.); for zú--kéše(-d^{r} [*kešed^{r}/ kšed^{r}]) see A. Cavigneaux/F. Al-Rawi, ZA 85 (1995) 36f.

4.1.2 Akkadian

ilum (diĝir)	(a) god
-ma	and
mālikum (ad-ge_4-ge_4)	counsellor; adviser
puḫrum (unken)	assembly; council
rīmum	gift
šemûm (ĝeš--tuku)	to hear
šu (cf. lú)	the one who belongs to (in proper names of the *šu*-DN type)
u (-bi-da)	and
ummum (ama)	mother

4.1.3 Amorite

ḫammu(*m*) [*'ammu*(*m*)]	paternal uncle ("grandfather" according to J.M. Durand, CRRA 38 [1992] 120, note 174)
rāpi'u(*m*)	healing (see M.P. Streck, AOAT 271/1, 207f.)

4.2 Divine Names

Each name is accompanied by:

1) *Its etymology;* 2) *The chief cult place;* 3) *The god's main characteristics.*

^{d}**ama-ušumgal-an-na**: 1) For the latest study of this name see M. Fritz, AOAT 307, 269-271; M. Krebernik, Studies Wilcke, 153-156; 166-167; 3) Associated with Lugaluru(b) in pre-Sargonic Lagas; eventually assimilated to Dumuzi.

^{d}**amar-**^{d}***zuen***: A (deified) ruler during the Ur III period.

an: 1) "Heaven"; 2) Uruk; 3) Personification of the heavens; nominal head of the Sumerian pantheon.

ánzu(-d)^{mušen}: 1) For the latest study of this name see B. Alster, RA 85 (1991) 1-5; 3) Personification of the storm-cloud, represented as a white eagle. Anzu stole the Tablet of Destinies from Enlil, but Ningirsu vanquished him, returned the Tablet to Enlil, and thus became his ur-sag̃ kala-ga.

^{d}**ba-Ú**: 2) Goddess of Iriku(-g) in G̃irsu (see G.J. Selz, UGASL, 26-103); 3) Vegetation goddess; Ning̃irsu's wife. For the writing variants of this name, which reflect different spellings in different periods, see G. Rubio, JCS 62 (2010) 35-43.

^{d}***da-gan***: 2) The region of Mari; 3) The West-Semitic storm-god, originally a chthonic god (see D.R. Frayne, BCSMS 25 [1993] 40 with notes 31-41).

^{d}**da-mu**: 3) A god of healing; one of the disappearing and dying gods whose sister goes to search for him.

^{d}**dumu-zi**(-d): 1) "'Noble' Child" (see M. Fritz, AOAT 307, 271f.; M. Kebernik, Studies Wilcke, 151-153); 2) God of Badtibira; 3) There are two traditions: one about Dumuzi the fisherman and one about Dumuzi the sheperd. The fisherman is from Ku'ara, the shepherd from Badtibira. The latter is also Inana's "husband" whom she sends to the underworld as a substitute for herself. He is the archetypal disappearing and dying god.

^{d}**dumu-zi-abzu**: 1) "'Noble' Child of the Abyss"; 2) Kinuniršа; 3) This divinity was generally regarded as female. At Eridu, however, the deity was considered male and formed part of Enki's entourage.

^{d}**en-ki**(-g/-k): 1) "Lord of the Earth"; 2) Eridu; 3) The crafty god of magic and wisdom; the helper of mankind. This divinity should be distinguished from **en-ki** "Lord Earth", one of the gods who existed before the separation of heaven and earth.

^{d}**en-líl**: 1) "Lord Breeze" is a popular etymology. What *e/illil really means is unknown (see X. Wang, AOAT 385, 6-19); 2) Nippur; 3) The *de facto* head of the Sumerian pantheon.

^{d}***èr-ra***: 3) A Semitic warrior and plague god who is associated with underworld deities.

^{d}**eš$_{5}$-peš**: 2) Adab; 3) A divinity found in third-millennium god-lists from Fara and Abū-Ṣalabīkh, as well as Early Dynastic and Early Sargonic mythological texts (see B. Alster/ A. Westenholz, ASJ 16 [1994] 37).

^{d}***eš$_{18}$-tár***: 3) Save for the absence of the sacred marriage, she was the Semitic equivalent of Inana, with whom she was syncretized.

^{d}**g̃á-tùm-du$_{10}$**(-g): 2) Lagas (see G.J. Selz, UGASL, 134-136; H. Steible, Studies Sjöberg, 507-513); 3) The mother-goddess at Lagas; special protectress of Gudea.

^{d}**ig-alim**: 1) "Door of the Bison" (see G.J. Selz, UGASL, 144-146); 2) Lagas; 3) Sul-Šagana's twin brother; the son of Ba'U and Ning̃irsu.

^{d}**inana**: 1) "Lady of Heaven" is a popular etymology; 2) Uruk; 3) The planet Venus; the heavenly courtesan; a warrior goddess; a vegetation goddess whose sacred marriage to Dumuzi, repeated every New Year's Day, guaranteed Sumer's fertility. She was syncretized with the Semitic E/Ištar and was most commonly thought to be the daughter of Nanna-*Zuen*. Regarding her relationship to An, the god of the sky, see J. van Dijk, Studies Borger, 9-11; 30.

^{d}**iškur**: 2) Karkara; 3) The storm-god.

^{d}***iš-me-^{d}da-gan***: A (deified) ruler during the Ur III period.

^{d}**ištaran**: 2) Dēr; 3) A god associated with judgement.

^{d}**lugal-uru$_{11}$**^{ki}(-b): 1) "King of Uru(b)" (see P. Pisi, OrAntMisc 2 [1995] 1-40; G.J. Selz, UGASL, 163-169); 2) Uru(b); 3) Syncretism identifies him with Inana's husband Dumuzi.

^{d}***marduk***: 1) The interpretation and milieu of the name *Marud/tuk (cf. the biblical Merōdaḫ) remain unclear. Certainly it is not, as popular etymology would have it, "bull-calf of the sun god" (see M. Krebernik, Studies Wilcke, 166f., note 128; for a different view of the etymology of this name according to a diachronic analysis see W.G. Lambert, Babylon, 73-76); 2) Babylon; 3) Chief god of Babylon and, during the first millennium, head of the whole pantheon as a result of his victory over Tiamat.

^{d}**namma**: 3) In the cosmogony of Eridu, the goddess who personified the primordial waters.

^{d}**nanna**: 2) Ur; 3) The Sumerian moon-god. His en-priestess lived in the G̃epar at Karzida in Ur and was a major personage in Sumerian religious life. The god was identified with *Zuen/Sîn*, the Semitic moon-god.

^{d}**naše**: 2) Nig̃en (see G.J. Selz, UGASL, 181-212); 3) Ning̃irsu's sister; interpreter of dreams; protectress of birds and fish; goddess of "social justice".

^{d}**nin-a-zu**: 1) "Lord Physician"; 2) Enegi; 3) An underworld god of healing; Ning̃ešzida's father.

^{d}**nin-dar**: 2) Ki'eš; 3) Naše's husband. The reading dar (not gùn) in the second part of the name is discussed by M. Civil, Studies Sjöberg, 50.

^{d}**nin-g̃eš-zi-da**: 1) "Lord of the True Tree"; 2) G̃ešbanda; 3) Ninazu's son; an underworld snake-god; Gudea's patron god. The latter seemingly introduced him into the Lagas pantheon to justify his own assumption of power.

^{d}**nin-g̃ír-su**: 1) "Lord of G̃irsu" (see G.J. Selz, UGASL, 218-251); 2) G̃irsu; 3) Ba'U's husband; he became Enlil's hero when he recovered the Tablet of Destinies that Anzu had stolen.

^{d}**nin-ḫur-sag̃**: 1) "Lady of the Mountain-Range"; 2) Keš (as well as in cities such as Adab; see M. Krebernik, RlA 8, 511f.); 3) A mother-goddess. Her name indicates where she appears. She is the creator of gods and men.

^{d}**nin-líl**: 1) "Lady Breeze" (popular etymology analogous to ^{d}en-líl "Lord Breeze"); 2) Nippur; 3) Enlil's wife.

^{d}**nin-MAR.KI**: 1) "Lady of Marg/ki"(?); see P. Attinger, N.A.B.U. 1995/33; 2) Guabba; 3) Naše's daughter.

^{d}**nin-subur**: 1) "Lord/Lady of (the land of) Subur/Subar"(?); 2) Akkil; 3) When male, An's high court official; when female, Inana's high court official.

^{d}**nin-te-ug$_5$-ga**: 1) By popular etymology "Lady who Keeps the Dying Alive" (usually written ^{d}nin-tin-ug$_5$-ga); compare Marduk's epithet *muballiṭ mīti*; 3) A goddess of healing.

^{d}**nin-tu**(-r): 1) "Lady birth-hut"(?); see Th. Jacobsen, OrNS 42 (1973) 274-298; A. Cavigneaux/M. Krebernik, RlA 9, 507f.); 2) Keš (as well as in cities such as Adab; see M. Krebernik, RlA 8, 511f.); 3) A mother-goddess. She is the creator of gods and men.

^{d}**nu-muš-da**: 2) Kazallu.

^{d}**nun-gal**: 1) "Great Nobility"; 2) Nippur; 3) A goddess associated with justice and judgement, especially the judicial ordeal.

^{d}**NUNUS.KAD$_4$**^{mušen}: 3) The determinative mušen shows that the divinity is a bird (see N. Veldhuis, CM 22, 277).

^{d}**sul-luḫša**: 2) Lagas; 3) Dynastic god of the rulers of Lagas from Urnašše to Enmetena. The reading and interpretation of this divine name is not entirely certain (see D.R. Frayne, RIME 1, 81f.).

^{d}**sul-šà-ga-na**: 1) "The Lad of his (Ninĝirsu's) Heart" (see G.J. Selz, UGASL, 277-279); 2) Lagas; 3) Igalim's twin brother; the son of Ba'U and Ninĝirsu.

^{d}**šára**: 2) Umma; 3) Inana's son; her manicurist and hair-dresser.

^{d}**utu**: 1) "Sun"; 2) Sippar; 3) The sun-god.

^{d}***zuen*** > ^{d}***sîn***: 1) The original meaning of this name is uncertain (see M. Krebernik, RlA 8, 362f.). According to D.R. Frayne, BCSMS 25 (1993) 40, it might go back to a Proto-Indo-European root; 2) Ur; 3) The Semitic moon-god identified with Nanna, the Sumerian moon-god.

For further reading see:

J. Black/A. Green, *Gods, Demons and Symbols of Ancient Mesopotamia. An Illustrated Dictionary* (London 1992).
G. Leick, *A Dictionary of Ancient Near Eastern Mythology* (London/New York 1991).
Th. Richter, *Untersuchungen zu den lokalen Panthea Süd- und Mittelbabyloniens in altbabylonischer Zeit* (Münster 2004 [= AOAT 257]).
G.J. Selz, *Untersuchungen zur Götterwelt des altsumerischen Stadtstaates von Lagaš* (Philadelphia 1995 [= OPSNKF 13]).

The relevant articles in the Reallexikon der Assyriologie (RlA).
For the Lagas pantheon of the Gudea period: the relevant articles in A. Falkenstein, *Die Inschriften Gudeas von Lagaš. I. Einleitung* (Rome 1966 [= AnOr 30]).

4.3 Personal Names

(Parentheses indicate the text in which the name appears)

a-ba-^{d}utu-gen$_{7}$ (30:4)
a-kur-gal (15 I 4; 16 II 1). A ruler of pre-Sargonic Lagas.
á-lu$_{5}$-lu$_{5}$ (38:26)
ad-da-šu-sikil (34 VI 1)
ama-iri (35:8). Possibly the name of a profession.
^{d}amar-^{d}*zuen* (27:4, 19, 25). A (deified) ruler of Ur in the Ur III period.
ba-ši-šà-ra-ge (32:3)
BU-KA (36:9)
diğir-a-ğu$_{10}$ (33 IV 2)
du-du (38:4, 6, 7, 12, 16, 18, 20, 22, 28, 34, 40, 43)
du-du-ú (36:12)
é-an-na-tum (16 I 1; III 9). A ruler of pre-Sargonic Lagas.
é-me-lim$_{4}$-sù (34 III 3)
en-an-na-túm (I) (14:13; 15 I 1; 20:10; 21 r.sh. I 1; I 10). A ruler of pre-Sargonic Lagas.
en-an-na-túm (II) (19:3, 16). A ruler of pre-Sargonic Lagas.
en-ig-gal (34 V 4; 40 II 1; 42 III 2; 44 II 4)
^{d}en-líl-lá-an-zu (36:10)
en-lú (34 VI 6)
en-šu (34 V 6)
en-te:me-na [= en-me-te-na] (11:1; 13:3; 8; 14:3; 19:10; 20:3, 20; 31; 21 r.sh. II 2; I 3; III 8, 11; IV 2, 7). A ruler of pre-Sargonic Lagas. For the reading of this name see D.R. Frayne, RIME 1, 193.
[^{d}]*èr-ra-ma-lik* (39:3)
^{d}*eš$_{18}$-tár-um-mi* (39:1)
gan-ki (34 II 5)
géme-^{d}ig-alim (37:15)
géme-^{d}nun-gal (31:4)
géme-ti-ra-áš (38:36)
gi-zi (38: 25)
gu-NI-DU (12 I 4). The father(?) of ur-^{d}našše, a ruler or high official of pre-Sargonic Lagas (see D.R. Frayne, RIME 1, 81).
gù-dé-a (2:3; 4:3; 5:3; 6:4; 7:4; 8:4; 9:4; 10:6; 22 r.sh. 1; I 5; III 7; 23 I 2; II 4, 14; III 18; 24 r.sh. 1; I 5; IV 4; V 5; 25 r.sh. 1; I 3; II 6; 26 I 7; III 4). A ruler of Lagas whose time of reign is uncertain. Perhaps he should be placed in the period between the Gutian dynasty and the beginning of Ur III.
ğešgal-si (34 II 6)
ḫa-am-mu-ra-pí (28:1, 21, 32). A ruler of Babylon in the Old-Babylonian Period.
ì-lí-A.Z[U] (39:2)
ì-lí-DIĞIR^{lum} (36:7)

⌜inim-lugal⌝ (37:13)
in-na-sa_6-ga (38:3, 8, 10, 13, 16, 21, 34, 40)
iri-KA-gi-na (17:3; 18 I 3; IV 5). A ruler of pre-Sargonic Lagas; for the latest discussion on the reading of this name see D.R. Frayne, RIME 1, 245f.
IŠ (30:13)
[^{d}*iš-m*]*e*-^{d}*da-gan*-zi-$\tilde{g}u_{10}$ (39:28)
$ka_5{}^{a}$ (36:13)
la-la (34 V 2; VII 2)
lú-^{d}da-mu (36:14)
lú-diğir-ra (32:10; 37:21; 38:49)
lú-$\tilde{g}u_{10}$ (32:7)
lú-ib-gal (37:20)
lú-^{d}inana (36:1)
lú-^{d}iškur (31:9)
lú-^{d}nin-subur (36:15)
lú-sa_6-ga (36:2)
lú-^{d}šára (32:8; 37:9, 19; 38:48)
lugal-á-gur-ra (34 II 1)
lugal-á-zi-da (31:3)
lugal-an-da (34 IV 2; 43 II 3). A ruler of pre-Sargonic Lagas.
lugal-da (33 III 3)
[l]ugal-eden-né (34 I 1)
lugal-ḫé-ğál (31:10)
lugal-igi-ḫuš (37:8)
lugal-iti-da (36:17)
lugal-ki-gal-la (37:5)
lugal-KU (30:11)
lugal-níğ-zu (35:1)
lugal-ra-mu-ge_4 (34 VI 8)
ma-gi-na (38:37)
munus-kur-ra (43 I 2)
nam-ḫa-ni (36:8)
nam-maḫ (38:25)
^{d}našše:ur, see ur-^{d}našše.
ni-za (38:15, 32, 39)
níğ-gur_{11} (35:9)
níğ-ú-rum (37:2, 9, 11, 12, 16)
nin-a-na (38:15, 39)
nin-inim-zi-da (35:3)
$para_{10}$-nam-tar-ra (34 IV 1). The wife of Lugalanda, a pre-Sargonic ruler of Lagas. Formerly read bára-nam-tar-ra.
pú-ta (31:10)
ri-im-^{d}*sîn* (29 I 13). A ruler of Larsa in the Old-Babylonian Period.
sa_6-sa_6 (44 VII 1). The wife of IriKAgina, a ruler of pre-Sargonic Lagas.

sag̃-^{d}ba-Ú-tuku (38:38)
ses-lú-du$_{10}$ (40 I 2)
ses-sa$_{6}$-ga (44 VI 5)
šà-šu-níg̃en (32:2)
šu-duran ([DUR$^{!}$.KIB] 31:5)
^{d}*šu-*^{d}*sîn* (32:12). A (deified) ruler of Ur in the Ur III period.
ti-ti (38:4)
ú-šè-ḫé-DU (32:2)
ur-ba-gára (38:47)
ur-^{d}ba-Ú (37:8)
ur-du$_{6}$ (42 II 1)
ur-^{d}dumu-zi (43 III 3)
ur-é-mùš (33 I 3; 34 VI 3)
ur-é-ninnu (38:7)
ur-^{d}eš$_{5}$-peš (30:2)
ur-gu-la (38:24)
ur-^{d}ig-alim (32:7; 37:6)
ur-^{d}inana (35:7)
ur-^{d}iškur (31:2, 7)
ur-^{d}ištaran (32:9; 37:18, 22; 38:50)
ur-kèš^{ki} (30:6)
ur-ki (33 II 4)
ur-^{d}namma (1:3; 3:3). A ruler of Ur in the Ur III period.
ur-^{d}našše 1) A ruler of pre-Sargonic Lagas (12 I 1 [written: ^{d}našše:ur]; 21 I 14); formerly read ur-^{d}nanše. 2) A party in a wedding contract (32:3).
ur-nig̃ar$^{g̃ar}$ (36:11)
ur-^{d}nin-MAR.KI (41 II 2)
ur-^{d}<nu->muš-da (37:2)
ur-^{d}NUNUS.KAD$_{4}$^{mušen} (38:47)
ur-zu (35:6); ur-zu$^{!}$ (35: 4)
ur-^{d}*zuen* (31:8)
úrdu-^{d}nanna (38:19)
utu-lú-g̃u$_{10}$ (34 III 2)

For further information on these names see:

R.A. Di Vito, *Studies in Third Millennium Sumerian and Akkadian Personal Names. The Designation and Conception of the Personal God* (Rome 1993 [= St.Pohl SM 16]).
J. Andersson, *Kingship in the Early Mesopotamian Onomasticon 2800-2200 BCE* (Uppsala 2012 [= St.Sem.Ups. 28]).

4.4 Place Names

ararma[ki]: The Sumerian city of the sun-god. It ruled Sumer in Old-Babylonian times between the fall of Isin and the rise of Babylon, when it was known as larsa(m)[ki] (see D. Arnaud, RlA 6, 496 § 1).

i7**buranuna** (*purattu*) [28:16]: The Euphrates. For the interpretation of the different writings of this important Mesopotamian watercourse see C. Woods, ZA 95 (2005) 7-32.

delmun[ki]: The region between what is today Falaika and Baḫrain.

(i7)***duran*** [31:5]: The river Diyāla. See D.O. Edzard, RGTC 1, 210. For the reading *d/tur(r)an* (DUR.KIB/ÙL) see MSL X, 26-27; K. Nashef, BaM 13 (1982) 120, note 15; 133f., note 72.

é-GUM.DÚR(-ra) [38:2, 33]: Meaning and reading unknown.

elam[ki]: The region in south-western Iran with Susa as its centre. It was hereditary enemies with Lagas.

eridu[ki](-g): A city in Sumer and the centre of Enki's cult. The name seems to mean "Good City".

gu-bi[ki](-n): The location of this land, mentioned in 25 IV 9 in the sequence Magan, Meluḫḫa, Gubi, and Delmun, is uncertain (see D.T. Potts, N.A.B.U. 1996/65).

gú-eden-na: "The Border of the Steppe"; the boundary between Lagas and Umma, object of constant war between the two states. See H.J. Nissen, AS 20, 34f.

g̃ír-su[ki]: An important settlement that was part of the city-state of Lagas (see D.R. Frayne, RIME 1, 77). Its god was Ning̃irsu.

IM-KA-ZI/ZI.ŠÈ: A place mentioned in 21 r.sh. I 2 whose reading is uncertain (see J. Bauer, AoN 1987, 6, n. 39; id., WO 30 [1999] 171 and WO 39 [2009] 251; according to G. Marchesi/N. Marchetti, MC 14, 178, the term should be read and interpreted as ní-zú-šub$_5$ [field named] "Thief of Rushes").

im-sag̃ (18 III 9): While this may be the name of a place, the location of Enlil's temple é-ad-da, it could just as likely be the temple's epithet. It is discussed in H. Steible/H. Behrens, FAOS 5/2, 109f., note 15.

iri-kù(-g): "Shining City". A quarter in G̃irsu where the temple of Ba'U was located (see A. Falkenstein, AnOr 30, 121f.; for other early evidence of this toponym see V. Crawford, Iraq 36 [1974] 29-35).

KÁ.DIĞIR.RA[ki]: "Gate of God". This Sumerogram for the name of Babylon is a popular etymology based on the Semitic *bāb ilim*. For the history of this place name see B. Kienast, Sumer 35 (1979) 246-248; W.G. Lambert, Babylon, 71-73.

ká-sur-ra (24 III 6): "Boundary Gate" where kar-za-gìn, "The Lapis-lazuli Quay" was located. It is not clear where ká-sur-ra was exactly located.

kar-nun (24 III 4): "Princely Quay". Ba'U's magur-boat is associated with this place (24 III 3).

kar-silim-ma (28:19): "Quay of Well-Being"; located at Zimbir.

kar-za-gìn (24 III 6): "Lapis-lazuli Quay" or "Pure Quay"; located at ká-sur-ra.

kar-zi-da (27:15): "The True Quay". At Ur, the location of the G̃epar where Nanna's en-priestess lived.

ki-en-gi(-r) (*keĝir): "Native Land". The Sumerian's own name for their land (see C. Wilcke, CRRA 19 [1974] 202-232; P. Steinkeller, HANE/S 5, 112, note 9; id., Studies Klein, 305-310; J.S. Cooper, RlA 13, 290-297).

ki-lagas[ki] (29:17): The city-state of Lagas. Its main settlements were Lagas, G̃irsu, and Niĝen(-Sirara); see M. Yoshikawa, ASJ 7 (1985) 157-164; D.R. Frayne, RIME 1, 77-79.

ki-uri: The Sumerian name for the land of Akkade. uri is the Sumerian rendering of the Semitic *war*(*i*) (see P. Steinkeller, HANE/S 5, 115f., note 18).

lagas[ki]: The settlement Lagas (formerly read lagaš[ki]) in the state of the same name (see M. Yoshikawa, ASJ 7 [1985] 157-164; D.R. Frayne, RIME 1, 77f.).

má-gan[ki]: A region corresponding to modern Oman; the source of precious metals, stone, and wood (see W. Heimpel, RlA 7, 195-199).

me-luḫ-ḫa[ki]: In the third and early second millennium this was probably the settlement area of the Mohenjo-Daro civilization (see W. Heimpel, RlA 8, 53-55).

nibru[ki] (*nippuru*): Enlil's city, the religious centre of Sumer (see J. Klein, RlA 9, 532-539).

niĝen$_6$[ki]: A settlement in the state of Lagas whose goddess was Našše (see D.O. Edzard, RlA 9, 322-324).

pa$_5$-kù(-g) [21 r.sh. I 4]: "Shining Canal"; located near Niĝen.

pa$_5$-sír-ra (21 II 11): "Broad Canal", where Enmetena built an Abzu for Enki (see D.O. Edzard, RGTC 1, 136f.; J. Bauer, WO 30 [1999] 171).

si-ma-núm^{ki} (38:51): A city located near modern Mardin in south-eastern Turkey; it was destroyed in *Šu-Sîn*'s third year.

su$_{11}$-lum (21 II 7): The location of Našše's temple é-engur-ra, "House of the Subterranean Waters" (see D.O. Edzard, RGTC 1, 147).

subur: Subartu, the land north of Mesopotamia; it seemingly appears in the name of the divinity ^{d}nin-subur (see *Divine Names*).

sur-^{d}našše (21 r.sh. I 1): "Border of Našše". Its location is unknown; according to J.S. Cooper, SARI I, 64 n. 5 (ad La 5.17) "it is unclear if this is a personal or a geographical name". G. Marchesi/N. Marchetti, MC 14, 178 propose a reading /aš$_{11}$-né/ instead of /sur/. The field name would then be read as en-an-na-túm-aš$_{11}$-né-^{d}našše-e-ta-e$_{11}$.

ter-kù(-g) (21 II 15): "Shining 'Forest'". The location of Ninḫursag̃'s gi-gù-na that Enmetena built.

umma^{ki}: A Sumerian city, the hereditary enemy of Lagas. For the Sumerogram (G̃IŠ.KÚŠU. KI) of this toponym a reading /g̃iša^{ki}/ has been proposed by G.J. Selz, Studies Kienast, 508 and D.R. Frayne, RIME 1, 357-359. This has been forcefully rejected by G. Marchesi/ N. Marchetti, MC 14, 170f.

unug^{ki} (*uruk*): The city of An and Inana.

úri^{ki}(-m) (also **uri$_{5}$**^{ki}(-m)): Nanna's city; Eannatum conquered it (16 II 10). It became the capital of the Ur III Dynasty that ruled Sumer and Akkad during the last century of the third millennium.

uru$_{11}$^{ki}(-b): A settlement in the state of Lagas. In text 20 it is mentioned in connection with offerings to its god Lugaluru(b). For the reading of this place name see K. Volk, N.A.B.U. 1997/60.

uru$_{18}$^{ki}: A city conquered by Eannatum (16 II 6). For a possible reading /*urua/ see P. Steinkeller, ZA 72 (1982) 244f., note 26-27.

zimbir^{ki} (*sippa/ir*) [28:17]: The city of the sun-god where Ḫammurapi built a canal.

For particulars about each place, see the appropriate entry in RGTC 1 and 2.

4.5 Sacred Buildings

a-ḫuš (21 I 20): Syllabic writing of é-ḫuš, "Fearsome House". Ninĝirsu's sanctuary built by Enmetena (*Gazetteer, n. 491*).

abzu: It is usually written ZU.AB, as in 37:24; but in 36:20 it is written ab-zu. It is Enki's underwater dwelling. The word refers to a cultic structure. In 41 I 4 it stands for Enki's sanctuary in Pasirra (*Gazetteer, n. 31*).

an-ta-sur-ra (18 II 1; 21 II 18): "(House) which Twinkles from Heaven". Ninĝirsu's sanctuary, dating to at least the time of Urnašše (*Gazetteer, n. 83*).

ba-gára (in our texts it appears only in the personal name ur-ba-gára [38 IV 47]): Ninĝirsu's sanctuary in Lagas (*Gazetteer, n. 96*).

bur-saĝ (18 IV 2): "Foremost Jar". A building that seems to have served as a pantry (see G.J. Selz, SEL 13 [1996] 3-8). Its epithet is é-sá-du_{11}-an-na-ta$^{!}$-ÍL-a-ni "His House from which Regular Offerings are delivered to him (Ninĝirsu)" (*Gazetteer, n. 129*).

é-ad-da (18 III 8; 21 r.sh. II 6; I 2; IV 3): "House of the Father". The sanctuary of Enlil, Ninĝirsu's father. Its exact location is unknown (*Gazetteer, n. 40*).

é-an-na (23 I 5; IV 3): "House of Heaven", Inana's temple in G̃irsu. It probably owed its name to the é-an-na in Uruk, Inana's most important cultic centre (*Gazetter n. 77*).

é-ánzu^{mušen}-bábbar (8:8): "House, White Anzu". The name of this temple is attested only on brick inscriptions found at G̃irsu, Tell I (see A. Falkenstein, AnOr 30, 121; 123, a-ga-erena).

é-^{d}ba-Ú (18 III 5): "Temple of Ba'U", rebuilt by IriKAgina (see J. Bauer, AWL, 198f. ad 46 III 2; id., OBO 160/1, 478).

é-bábbar (17:2): "White House". This is not Utu's famous temple in Zimbir/*Sippar*, but a temple in the state of Lagas. According to G.J. Selz, FAOS 15/1, 194, it was dedicated to Ninĝirsu (*Gazetteer, n. 99*).

é-BI×NÍĜ (18 II 6; 19:14): "House of Beer-Bread" (formerly read é-bàppir); the brewery, part of the é-ninnu where it seems beer was brewed. Its epithet was ĝeštin$^{!}$ sìla-gal-[gal] kur-ta de_6-a "(to which) Grape Juice Has Been Brought in 'Big' Litre-Vessels from the Mountain Regions".

é-engur-ra (21 II 7): "House of the Subterranean Waters". Naššе's temple located in Sulum near Lagas, built by Enmetena (*Gazetteer, n. 250*).

é-gal-ti-ra-áš (18 I 8): "Palace of Tiraš". Ninĝirsu's sanctuary dating to at least the time of Urnašše (*Gazetteer, n. 1097*).

é-gal-uru$_{11}$^{ki}(-b) [20:22; 21 II 4]: "Palace of Uru(b)". Temple of Lugal-uru(b), located in Uru(b) (*Gazetteer, n. 1351*).

é-^{ĝeš}**gígir** (13:6; 18 II 3): "Chariot House". Part of the é-ninnu where Ninĝirsu's chariot was kept (see A. Falkenstein, AnOr 30 126f., 15). Its epithet was é me-lim$_4$-bi kur-kur-ra dul$_5$ (18 II 4) "House whose Splendour Covers the Mountains" (*Gazetteer, n. 766*).

é-^{d}**ĝá-tùm-du$_{10}$**(-g) [21 II 22]: "Ĝatumdu's temple", located in Iriku in Ĝirsu (*Gazetteer, n. 1314*).

é-$^{ĝeš\text{-}tu_9}$**ĝeštu-šu-du$_7$** (29:25): "House that Perfects Understanding". Enki's temple in Ur (*Gazetteer, n. 364*).

é-ĝidru (10 rev. 3; 24 II 11): "House of the Sceptre", a seven-cornered house (é ub umun$_7$). Part of the é-ninnu (*Gazetteer, n. 393*).

é-iri-kù-ga (10 rev. 5; 26 III 7): "House of the Shining City". Temple of Ba'U in the sacred quarter of Ĝirsu (*Gazetteer, n. 1198*).

é-^{d}**lugal-uru$_{11}$**(-b)^{ki} [20:32]: "Temple of Lugaluru(b)", located in Uru(b) (*Gazetteer, n. 1351*).

é-maḫ (22 II 5): "Sublime House". While this is the name of Ninḫursaĝ's temple in Ĝirsu, it is uncertain whether our passage refers to the temple by name, or whether the phrase simply means "sublime house" (*Gazetteer, n. 716*).

é-me-ḫuš-gal-an-ki (18 III 3) "House of the Great Furious Me of Heaven and Earth/ Underworld". Igalim's temple in Ĝirsu (*Gazetteer, n. 755*).

é-mùš (in the PN ur-é-mùš, 33 I 3; 34 VI 3): "House, Foundation (of the Land)". Dumuzi's temple in Badtibira (*Gazetteer, n. 829*).

é-ninnu (5:6; 10 rev. 1; 22 r.sh. 4; 23 II 8; 24 V 9; PN ur-é-ninnu 38:7) also called é-ninnu-ánzu^{mušen}-bábbar (7 II 2; 24 II 7; 25 I 9): "House-Fifty" and "House-Fifty, White Anzu". The most important sacred building in the state of Lagas, it was Ninĝirsu's temple complex in Ĝirsu. Its name shows that it housed the fifty 'me'. This is apparent from Gudea, cylinder A X 6. According to D.O. Edzard, CM 7, 160, note 6 and J. Bauer, WO 30 (1999) 171 though, this interpretation remains doubtful. The temple dates to the time of Mesalim of Kiš (see J. Bauer, OBO 160/1, 446) but was substantially rebuilt by Gudea (*Gazetteer, n. 897*).

é-sá-du$_{11}$-an-na-ta$^!$**-ÍL-a-ni** (18 IV 3): "His House from which Regular Offerings are Delivered to Him (Ninĝirsu)". Epithet of the bur-saĝ.

é-šu-sì-ga (29:29): "Cella", "Temple Chamber"; Part of Enki's temple é-g̃éštu-šu-du$_7$ in Ur.

é-tar-sír-sír (26 II 1; III 3): Temple of Ba'U. It was originally located in Lagas but transferred to G̃irsu by Gudea (*Gazetteer, n. 1086*).

èš-dug-ru (21 I 18): "Shrine (in which) Pots are Arranged" that belonged to Ning̃irsu (*Gazetteer, n. 1375*).

gi-gù-na (*gigunû*): A building ('reed chamber'; see H. Waetzoldt, Studies Klein, 323-329) constructed on a terrace for Ning̃irsu [11:4 (èš-gi gi-gù-na)] (*Gazetteer, n.* 1376); for Ninḫursag̃ in Terku(-g) [21 II 14]; for Našše [21 III 2] (*Gazetteer, n. 1362*).

gi-guna$_4$ (24 II 9): An alternate spelling of gi-gù-na. Here it designates the edifice located in the é-ninnu.

g̃e$_6$-par$_4$ (27:17, 21) "*Giparu*(-House)". The dwelling of the en-priestess of Nanna at Ur (*Gazetteer, n. 378*).

ib (*tubuqtu*; 44 I 7): "(Temple) 'Niche'"(?); see H. Behrens/H.Steible, FAOS 6, 167 s.v.

ib-gal (37:20, in PN lú-ib-gal): "Big 'Niche'"(?). Inana's temple complex (a temple oval; see J. Bauer, OBO 160/1, 443) in the city of Lagas (*Gazetteer, n. 505*).

ki-tuš-akkil-lé (18 II 9): "Abode of Lamentation". Sulšagana's shrine at G̃irsu (in the é-ninnu? – *Gazetteer, n. 618*).

ses-(e-)g̃ar-ra (14:2): "Established by the Brother (Ning̃irsu)". This refers to Našše's chapel in the Eninnu at G̃irsu. In our text it remains uncertain whether the phrase is the name of the temple é-ses-g̃ar-ra or just Našše's epithet (*Gazetteer, n. 1047*).

šà-pà-da (21 II 20): "(House) Called in the Heart", i.e. "Chosen House". Našše's temple in the city of Lagas (*Gazetteer, n. 1022*).

For further information about the buildings mentioned above see A.R. George, *House Most High. The Temples of Ancient Mesopotamia.* (Winona Lake 1993 [= MC 5]). '*Gazetteer*' in the Glossary refers to pp. 63-161 of this book.

4.6 Year Dates

Year dates of pre-Sargonic administrative texts

Text 33 = (Lugalanda) 6
Text 34 = (Lugalanda) 3
Text 40 = (IriKAgina) 2
Text 41 = (Lugalanda) 2
Text 42 = (IriKAgina) 2
Text 43 = (Lugalanda) 6
Text 44 = (IriKAgina) undated

For the dating system in these texts see no. 258 in the Sign List.

4.7 Year Names

For the year names in Ur III administrative texts, see the references in M. Sigrist/T. Gomi, *The Comprehensive Catalogue of Published Ur III Tablets* (Bethesda 1991). The writing variants of the individual year names are listed in N. Schneider, *Die Zeitbestimmungen der Wirtschaftsurkunden von Ur III* (Rome 1936), 30ff. ('4. Gimilsin' [= *Šusîn*]).

Text 31 = *Šusîn* 8 (see M. Sigrist/T. Gomi, Catalogue, 327)
Text 32 = *Šusîn* 6 (see M. Sigrist/T. Gomi, Catalogue, 327)
Text 36 = *Šusîn* 3a (see M. Sigrist/T. Gomi, Catalogue, 327)
Text 37 = *Šusîn* 2 (see M. Sigrist/T. Gomi, Catalogue, 326)
Text 38 = *Šusîn* 4a (M. Sigrist/T. Gomi, Catalogue, 327)

4.8 Festivals

Text 41: izim-amar-a-a-si-ge$_4$-da (see M.E. Cohen, Cultic Calendars, 58-60; G.J. Selz, UGASL, 258f. sub 8; J. Bauer, AfO 36/37 [1989/90] 88f.)
Text 42: izim-^{d}ba-Ú (see M.E. Cohen, Cultic Calendars, 53-54; G.J. Selz, UGASL, 70 sub 149, 72 sub 152)
Text 43: izim-še-gu$_7$-^{d}našše (see M.E. Cohen, Cultic Calendars, 44-46)
Text 44: izim-an-ta-sur-ra (see M.E. Cohen, Cultic Calendars, 56-57; G.J. Selz, UGASL, 240 sub 100; 242f. sub 110)